WM 203 BIR

| DATE DUE | | | |
|---|---|---|---|
| | | | |
| | | | |
| | | | |
| | | | |
| | | | |
| | | | |
| | | | |
| | | | |
| | | | |
| | | | |
| | | | |
| | | | |

LIBRARY & INFORMATION SERVICE

# Schizophrenia

Max Birchwood

Chris Jackson

*Early Intervention Service, Birmingham and University of Birmingham, UK*

Published in 2001 by Psychology Press Ltd
27 Church Road, Hove, East Sussex, BN3 2FA, UK

www.psypress.co.uk

Simultaneously published in the USA and Canada
by Taylor & Francis Inc
325 Chestnut Street, Suite 800, Philadelphia, PA 19106, USA

Reprinted 2001 by Psychology Press, Ltd
27 Church Road, Hove, East Sussex, BN3 2FA
29 West 35th Street, New York, NY 10001

*Psychology Press is part of the Taylor & Francis Group*

*British Library Cataloguing in Publication Data*
A catalogue record for this book is available from the British Library

*Library of Congress Cataloging-in-Publication Data*
A catalog record for this book is available from the Library of Congress

ISBN 0-86377-552-7 (hbk)
ISBN 0-86377-553-5 (pbk)
ISSN 1368-454X (Clinical Psychology: A Modular Course)

Cover design by Joyce Chester
Typeset in Palatino by Mayhew Typesetting, Rhayader, Powys
Printed and bound in the UK by TJ International Ltd, Padstow, Cornwall

In memory of Elaine Birchwood
and Gary Jackson

# Contents

# What is schizophrenia? 1

In this first chapter schizophrenia is defined and what it is like to suffer from the disorder is explained. Some of the controversies and difficulties surrounding the concept of schizophrenia are also discussed.

## The experience of schizophrenia

> . . . I sat down at home and my mother said I just started talking a load of utter rubbish . . . I was examined very thoroughly, but the doctors could not find anything wrong physically and put it all down to "nerves" . . . I avoided going out because people on the street could read my thoughts. My mind was transparent . . . I complained of hearing voices telling me to do different things, which I felt compelled to do . . . I felt everyone was against me, even the nurses and doctors . . . I did not clean my teeth, wash myself or comb my hair for the first two months . . . I just existed till I felt better when I gradually started to look after myself again. I used to sit all by myself and would hardly say anything to anyone . . .
>
> (Joe, a 22-year-old man diagnosed with schizophrenia)

Schizophrenia is a disorder of thinking where a person's ability to recognise reality, his or her emotional responses, thinking processes, judgement and ability to communicate deteriorates so much that his or her functioning is seriously impaired. Symptoms such as hallucinations and delusions are common.

(Warner, 1994, p. 4)

> . . . I saw the cross, and then God spoke to me. With this certainty my thoughts then took control. They were religious thoughts . . . and I began to hear an intermittent voice. Just prior to my acute admission, I announced to my aged father, who was in bed, Satan in the form of the Loch Ness Monster was going to land on the lawn and do it for us if we both remained together in the house. By this time, I heard the voice pretty constantly . . . the voice continued for four months. One day I was sitting listening to it when it suddenly said . . . . . . "This is the final transmission: over and out". I have never heard it since . . . again . . . my thoughts took control; it was a period of wildly erotic sensations, lack of sleep, being out walking at any time from 1.00am onwards, marked tiredness, and frequent ideas of reference. Messages were being transmitted by car registration numbers and many written sentences had messages hidden in them in code . . .
>
> (Errol, 26-year-old man with schizophrenia)

Delusions represent beliefs which are not shared by the individual's cultural peer group. In schizophrenia these tend to be of three main types. In the first, the individual may believe (and feel) that his or her behaviour is being influenced or controlled by some external force (delusions of influence or control). In the second, the person may believe he or she is being watched, followed or persecuted in some way (delusion of persecution). Finally, the individual may believe he or she has lost his sense of identity or purpose and may believe he or she has powers or abilities out of the ordinary (delusions of identity). The following description vividly portrays the experience of delusional identity and the acute distress that accompanies the lonely feeling of a delusion of persecution. This 23-year-old man worked as a storekeeper in a department store:

> . . . In my flat I began to get delusions. I was a storekeeper at the time. I wrote out a "supreme new plan", a system of life which I had worked out for myself . . . I wrote out notebooks full of plans. I kept thinking the Mafia were after me, and the FBI were protecting me, ready to send me away to be trained. I kept thinking my parents were Jews. I would ask my landlady, in my loneliness, if I could watch their television and I would cry all the way through the programmes. Finally, I tried to get away to my aunt

> Mary's: all I had with me was a suitcase with a bible in it. The Police picked me up and I made a false confession of murder so that they would incarcerate me and protect me from the Mafia . . . my doctor said I needed a rest. Sometime the next day, the medical superintendent and my mother came to certify me at the flat. A Social Worker took me to hospital. I didn't resist; I thought it was all part of the plan . . .
>
> (Mark, 23-year-old man with schizophrenia)

There is no doubt that people who are diagnosed with schizophrenia undergo a major change in mental and social functioning. For some these changes are transient, but in the majority of cases the changes are episodic or permanent.

Perhaps the greatest costs to the person affected by these experiences are the social and psychological consequences. It may, after all, be argued that there are many in society whose behaviour is statistically abnormal, yet who do not bring themselves, or are not brought by others, to public attention (Peters, Day McKenna, & Orbach, 1999). It is when such behaviour leads to a serious deterioration in the quality of life or results in danger to the well-being of the individual or others that the person concerned, his or her family, and society in general, feel a need to respond. Unemployment, social drift, social adversity, loss of confidence, drive, and even loss of the skills of independent living are among the most serious of these social and psychological effects. Once again, this is best illustrated by some actual case examples.

> . . . Colin works as a general labourer in a factory making garden tools. At nineteen years of age, he was living with his mother and sister in a council flat in a deprived area of the city. He had always been a quiet person with few friends. His interests were predominantly solitary (fishing, gardening) although he occasionally spent evenings out with his brother. One summer, after visiting a fortune teller at a local fair, Colin felt convinced that she had cast a spell upon him and that she exerted almost total control over his behaviour and thoughts. Colin became increasingly withdrawn and started to absent himself from work. He became suspicious of people, including his relatives that he thought were agents of the fortune teller. His mother reported that he spent much of the day in his bedroom

talking and laughing to himself. It was discovered that Colin was hearing voices which he thought was an attempt by the fortune teller to drive him insane.

The voices sometimes commented on his thoughts or behaviour ("he's going to sleep" [laughter]); sometimes they criticised him ("the way you act makes me sick"; "you're daft, I am") and sometimes they were bizarre or humorous ("he's not well liked but he's well liked", "monster crab claws for you old boy"). Colin refused to watch TV as he felt he heard thinly disguised references to him and his sanity. Colin's family had no previous acquaintance with such behaviour and at the time were resistant to identifying it as a mental illness, preferring to view it as a "phase" he was going through. Their perceptions changed suddenly when they realised that he had not eaten for three days and they called the family doctor who immediately admitted him to the local psychiatric hospital.

The following two months at the hospital Colin was much improved but he nonetheless continued to hear voices. He was unable to keep his job as the voices were too intrusive and distressing. At home, Colin withdrew further and his family were finding difficulty motivating him. Two years later Colin rarely laughs and seems to find it hard to understand what is said to him. He has given up the idea of working again and spends three days a week in a Day Centre. He spends much of the time alone in his room.

(Colin, a 24-year-old man diagnosed with schizophrenia)

Not everyone with schizophrenia, however, can be viewed as having an unfavourable outcome. Many (approximately 20%) will experience just one episode of psychotic symptoms in their entire life and return to a relatively normal existence. Even more (60%) will relapse more than once but will return to premorbid levels of functioning between episodes. Longitudinal prospective research studies throughout the world (e.g., Thara, Henrietta, Joseph & Eton, 1994), which overcome many of the bias sample effects in previous studies (i.e., tendency to follow up those in hospitals with the poorest outcomes), have concluded that a deterioration in schizophrenia is not inevitable. The advent of new drugs such as Clozapine, Olanzapine, and Risperidone as well as advances in psychosocial approaches, such as assertive community outreach, cognitive therapy, and early intervention (see Chapters 7 and 8) have meant that we are standing at the cusp of a new optimism in the treatment and management of schizophrenia. This is important because schizophrenia not only impacts upon the individual sufferers, but also upon those closest to them such as their families and on society in general, in terms of socio-economic costs.

## Schizophrenia and the family

> . . . She just sits there . . . she looks the same but she's not the same. She won't do anything unless I tell her. She often follows me around like a puppy which makes me lose my temper and then I feel guilty for shouting. I know they are doing all they can but they can't bring my daughter back. Sometimes my husband and I just want to cry.
>
> (Mother of 30-year-old woman [Sharon] with schizophrenia)

The vast majority (i.e. between 60% and 70%) of people with schizophrenia will return to live with their families, particularly in the early years following a first episode of psychosis (Stirling, Tantam, Thonks, Newby, & Montague, 1991). As we move away from hospital settings to more community-based approaches, families have an increasing role in the long-term care of their relatives with schizophrenia.

Such families are likely to encounter a range of problems which impact significantly upon family life. These will include withdrawal (staying in bed, emotional detachment, avoiding social contact); dealing with psychotic symptoms (i.e., persecutory delusions, hallucinatory behaviour); behavioural excesses (aggression, restlessness, and provocation of family discord), and impaired social performance (i.e., poor self care, domestic tasks, and independent skills).

Studies also describe the financial, physical, and psychological burden of caring for a relative with schizophrenia (Grad, & Sainsbury, 1968; Hatfield, 1978; see also Fadden, 1998).

Grief can be an understandable reaction to the changes sometimes brought about by schizophrenia (Birchwood, & Osborne, 2001). As illustrated in the previous example of the mother of Sharon, families may witness changes in social functioning and behaviours consistent with the "loss of a living relative" (Miller, 1996). This, of course, is not exclusive to schizophrenia or other forms of severe or enduring mental illness.

## The myths of schizophrenia

> [New York] . . . In January, Kendra Webdate, a young receptionist, was pushed to her death under a Manhattan subway train by a man who had stopped taking his medicine for schizophrenia. A month ago, both legs of Edgar Rivera, a father of 3, were severed by a rush hour subway train after he was shoved onto the tracks by a homeless man believed to be off his medication for schizophrenia.
>
> Earlier in April, New York police shot Charles Stevens eight times after he threatened them with the sword he was brandishing at commuters in Penn Station.
>
> Stevens, who survived the attack, had refused to take his medication for schizophrenia.
>
> (*Chicago Tribune*, Tuesday, 1 June 1999)

Unfortunately, much of our understanding and knowledge of schizophrenia is influenced by the media. Although many articles, reports, and TV programmes are undoubtedly informative, editing bias and selective abstraction on the part of the reader conspire to maintain many of the myths and stereotypes we hold about people with schizophrenia. As indicated in the quote from the *Chicago Tribune*, one of the major myths is that people with schizophrenia are disproportionately violent and aggressive unless sedated with powerful antipsychotic medication. Yet, if we examine the evidence for this in more detail, the truth is more complex. Modestin (1998), reviewing the literature on criminal and violent behaviour in people with schizophrenia, concludes that although there does appear to be a slightly elevated risk of aggression, much of this risk depends upon the nature of the symptoms (delusions, hallucinations, etc.) and whether or not illicit substances are involved. In reality, people with schizophrenia are much more likely to kill themselves than others (Allebeck, Varla, & Wistedt, 1986).

# Symptoms of schizophrenia

One of the most traditional methods of classifying mental illness is by dividing it into either neurosis or psychosis. The former usually refers to anxiety disorders (i.e., post traumatic stress disorder, obsessive compulsive disorder, generalised anxiety disorder, social anxiety, phobias, and panic disorder; see Rachman, 1998) and unipolar depression (see Hammen, 1997). It is argued that within the neuroses despite often suffering extreme levels of distress, a person's sense of reality remains intact. In psychosis it is believed that contact with reality is severely distorted (Cutting, & Charlish, 1995), even if this is only on a temporary basis. Schizophrenia is the most common and perhaps best known of the psychotic disorders. Related disorders such as schizophreniform disorder, schizoaffective disorder, delusional disorder, and brief psychotic disorder are differentiated diagnostically from schizophrenia on the basis of the nature and duration of the psychotic symptoms (see Hirsch, & Weinberger, 1995; McKenna, 1997 for a more detailed review). People with manic depression and chronic unipolar depression may also display psychotic features such as hallucinations and delusions (Goodwin, & Jamison, 1992; Sands, & Harrow, 1994).

Table 1.1 presents what most clinicians and researchers agree to be the main symptoms of schizophrenia. Although, as discussed previously, some of the symptoms may also be present in other disorders such as manic depression and other types of psychosis, it is argued that people with schizophrenia demonstrate a particular pattern and intensity of symptoms. This will be discussed in more detail in the next section, "Diagnosing schizophrenia".

Many of the symptoms described in Table 1.1 are illustrated by the case material at the beginning of the chapter. For instance, Joe felt compelled to do as his "voices" (auditory hallucinations) had told him; Errol's "voice" continued for 4 months before it announced "over and out" and was not heard again; Colin's hallucinations either commented on his thoughts and behaviour, criticised him, or made bizarre comments. Colin believed that a fortune teller had "cast a spell upon him" and therefore exerted control over his behaviour and thoughts (experiences of control).

Most of the case examples describe delusions. Joe, for example, felt everyone was against him including the doctors and nurses, whereas Mark believed the Mafia were after him (delusions of persecution). Delusions of reference are common: Errol, for instance, thought that

TABLE 1.1

**Main symptoms of schizophrenia**

**Auditory hallucinations**: false perceptions often in the form of noises or voices talking to each other about the person or commentating on his/her thoughts or actions in the third person.

**Experiences of control**: person feels under the control of an alien force or power. They may also experience the feeling that an external force has penetrated their mind or body. This is often interpreted as the presence of spirits, X-rays, or implanted radio transmitters.

**Delusions**: false personal beliefs about the world, which can take many different forms (i.e., persecutory, grandiose, reference, etc.). For instance, delusions of reference are beliefs held by the person that the behaviour and/or remarks of others (in the street, on TV, on the radio, etc.) are meant for them.

**Disorders of thinking**: the feeling that thoughts have been inserted or withdrawn from the mind. In some cases the person may feel that their thoughts are being broadcast so that others can hear them, often over long distances.

**Emotional and volitional changes**: emotions and feelings become blurred or less clear and are often described as being "flat". There may also be a loss of initiative or energy. Such changes are sometimes referred to as "negative symptoms".

messages relating to him were being transmitted by car registration numbers and written sentences (in coded form); Colin avoided watching TV as he believed that television programmes often made references about him and his sanity. Delusions may sometimes be interpretations of hallucinations: Errol thought God was speaking to him, and Colin believed his thoughts were an attempt by the fortune teller to drive him insane.

Disorders of thinking can also be witnessed in this previous case material. Joe describes the distress of thought broadcast ("people could read my thoughts") and how it may provoke avoidance and social withdrawal. After some time changes in emotion and volition may increase such social withdrawal as people struggle to energise themselves. This is clearly evident in Colin's case as his family struggle to motivate him and Colin struggles to recapture some of the emotions that were evident before the onset of the illness (i.e., being able to laugh).

In describing the changes that can occur with schizophrenia, Wing, a British social psychiatrist has argued that a distinction should be drawn between impairments which are intrinsic to the disorder (largely psychological) and those that are secondary, resulting from

**TABLE 1.2**

**Some common problems associated with schizophrenia**

**Intrinsic impairments**
    Persisting symptoms (hallucinations), delusions, thought disorders
    Tendency to withdrawal, apathy, emotional blunting ("negative" symptoms)
    Cognitive impairments: attention and problem-solving
    Vulnerability to further schizophrenic episodes

**Secondary impairments**
*Social*
    Unemployment, downwards social drift
    Social adversity: housing, finance, etc.
    Institutionalisation
    Diminished social network
    Family discord or rejection
    Social prejudice to mental illness
*Psychological*
    Loss of confidence and achievement motivation
    Social and community survival skills impaired or fall into disuse
    Dependent or semi-independent on family or institutions
    Distress due to poor coping with persisting symptoms (e.g., auditory
       hallucinations)

the interaction of primary impairments with the social environment. These are illustrated in Table 1.2.

Throughout this book reference will be made to these different levels of impairment, their causes and more importantly how one may intervene to reduce them.

# Diagnosing schizophrenia

There is no doubt that in the past the diagnosis of schizophrenia has been too widely and too liberally applied to a number of psychological and psychiatric difficulties. For instance, prior to 1970 there was a great difference in the prevalence rates of schizophrenia in different countries. Before 1970, American psychiatry employed a broad concept of schizophrenia, which included disorders that in European countries often attracted a diagnosis of manic depressive illness. Scandinavian psychiatry in contrast tended to exclude brief schizophrenic illnesses and place more emphasis on poor outcome cases (Warner, 1994). It also became apparent from studies looking at the reliability of psychiatrists' diagnostic practices that there was considerable disagreement between clinicians when diagnosing schizophrenia. As a result, attempts were made to standardise the criteria for the diagnosis of schizophrenia. This meant, in theory, that a psychiatrist diagnosing schizophrenia in one clinic would be more likely to be consistent with another psychiatrist diagnosing schizophrenia in another clinic.

Today there are three major diagnostic classification systems in use: *ICD-10* (World Health Organisation, 1992), *Diagnostic and Statistical Manual*, fourth edition (*DSM-IV*; American Psychiatric Association, 1994), and the *Research Diagnostic Criteria* (RDC; Spitzer, Endicott, & Robins, 1978). *ICD-10* is more common throughout Europe, whereas *DSM-IV* tends to be used more often in the United States. Although there are differences between these two systems, they also have much in common. For instance, they are similarly constructed in that they consist of a primary list of symptoms of which at least one must be present to make the diagnosis, and a second group of symptoms of which at least two must be present (Drake, Haddock, Hopkins, & Lewis, 1998).

The main difference between the *ICD* and the *DSM* criteria is in the amount of time the symptoms have to be present. In *DSM-IV* (Table 1.3) symptoms must be clearly present for most of the time during a period of *1 month*, whereas in *ICD-10* (Table 1.4) it is specified that there should be evidence of continuous disturbance persisting for *at least 6 months*.

The "Research Diagnostic Criteria" (Spitzer et al., 1978), which was a forerunner to the classificatory systems of *ICD* and *DSM*, was initially developed for research purposes. Its intention was to identify patients with a relatively similar group of symptoms but which avoided limiting the sample to those with a more chronic or deteriorating course (Drake, Haddock, Hopkins, & Lewis, 1998). Symptoms in the *RCD* diagnostic system should be present for at least 2 weeks.

In practice, psychiatrists often have to differentiate between schizophrenia and other related disorders on the basis of the quality and quantity of the symptoms reported by either the patient themselves and/or a relative or friend. A clear picture does not always emerge at first. Patients may deny their symptoms or be unwilling to discuss them. Accurate diagnosis may be especially difficult just after the first episode of psychotic symptoms (McGorry, Edwards, Michalopoulos, Harringan, & Jackson, 1996).

Although there is some good evidence to suggest that the reliability of diagnosing schizophrenia has improved over the last 20 years, a number of problems still remain. One of the difficulties in

**TABLE 1.3**

*DSM-IV*—diagnostic criteria for schizophrenia. Reprinted with permission from the Diagnostic and Statistical Manual of Mental Disorders, Fourth Edition. Copyright 1994 American Psychiatric Association

A. *Characteristic symptoms*: Two (or more) of the following, each present for a significant portion of time during a 1-month period (or less if successfully treated):

    (1) delusions
    (2) hallucinations
    (3) disorganised speech (e.g., frequent derailment or incoherence)
    (4) grossly disorganised or catatonic behaviour
    (5) negative symptoms, i.e., affective flattening, alogia, or avolition

Note: only one Criterion A symptom is required if delusions are bizarre or hallucinations consist of a voice keeping up a running commentary on the person's behaviour or thoughts, or two or more voices conversing with each other.

B. *Social/occupational dysfunction*: For a significant portion of the time since the onset of the disturbance, one or more major areas of functioning such as work, interpersonal relations, or self-care are markedly below the level achieved prior to the onset (or when the onset is in childhood or adolescence, failure to achieve expected level of interpersonal, academic, or occupational achievement).

C. *Duration*: Continuous signs of the disturbance persist for at least 6 months. This 6-month period must include at least 1 month of symptoms (or less if successfully treated) that meet Criterion A (i.e., active-phase symptoms) and may include periods of prodromal or residual symptoms. During these prodromal or residual periods, the signs of the disturbance may be manifested by only negative symptoms or two or more symptoms listed in Criterion A present in an attenuated form (e.g., odd beliefs, unusual perceptual experiences).

D. *Schizoaffective and mood disorder exclusion*: Schizoaffective disorder and mood disorder with psychotic features have been ruled out because either (1) no major depressive, manic, or mixed episodes have occurred concurrently with the active-phase symptoms; or (2) if mood episodes have occurred during active-phase symptoms, their total duration has been brief relative to the duration of the active and residual periods.

E. *Substance/general medical condition exclusion*: The disturbance is not due to the direct physiological effects of a substance (e.g., a drug of abuse, a medication) or a general medical condition.

F. *Relationship to a pervasive development disorder*: If there is a history of autistic disorder or another pervasive development disorder, the additional diagnosis of schizophrenia is made only if prominent delusions or hallucinations are also present for at least a month (or less if successfully treated).

TABLE 1.4

**ICD-10 diagnostic criteria for schizophrenia (with permission of the World Health Organization)**

A. One of the symptoms under A1
   Or two of the symptoms under A2
   Must be present for most of an episode lasting at least a month

   A1a. Thought echo, insertion, withdrawal, broadcasting
   A1b. Delusions of control, influence, passivity, delusional perception
   A1c. Verbal hallucinations, with running commentary or discussing
         patients or coming from a part of the body
   A1d. Delusions that are persistent and culturally implausible
   A2e. Persistent hallucinations with half-formed delusions without clear
         affective content.
   A2f. Breaks in train of thought, giving rise to incoherent or irrelevant
         speech, neologism
   A2g. Catatonic behaviour
   A2h. Negative-apathy, paucity of speech, blunted or incongruent affect, not
         due to depression or medication

B. If *manic or depressive episode*, Criterion A must be met *before* mood
   disturbance developed.

C. Not attributable to organic brain disease (FO) or substance misuse (F1).

All three conditions, A, B, and C must be satisfied.

diagnosing psychiatric disorders such as schizophrenia is that it forces people into categories which are not always mutually exclusive. According to these diagnostic systems it is not possible to have both schizophrenia and manic depression. Yet, as noted previously, manic depression may share some common features with schizophrenia as is evident in the following quote from Campbell (1953, p. 160):

> The impulsive, combative and irrational behaviour of the maniacal patient not infrequently is confused with . . . schizophrenia, particularly if the patient's delusional trend is at all bizarre or paranoid in nature.

For such reasons it is argued that careful attention should be given to what the patient was like before they became unwell for the first time (i.e., "premorbid" functioning), their family history of psychiatric illness, and the exact nature of their previous episodes of mental illness (Goodwin, & Jamison, 1992). Distinguishing between schizophrenia and an affective disorder (depression, mania, or hypomania) may also depend upon the degree and persistence of the mood

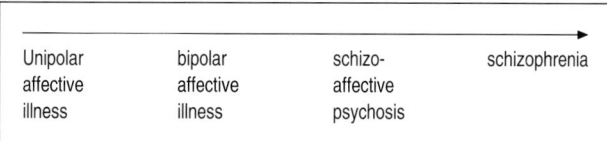

**Figure 1.1** The continuum view. From Crow T.J. (1986). The continuum of psychosis and its implications for the structure of the gene. *British Journal of Psychiatry, 149*, 425. Copyright © 1986 Royal College of Psychiatrists. Reprinted with permission

disorder and the relationship of symptoms such as hallucinations and delusions to the mood state (Gelder, Gath, & Mayou, 1989). Thus, delusions that are consistent with a person's mood (i.e., mood congruent) tend to be an indication of an affective disorder rather than schizophrenia. For example, a person who is depressed may have a strong belief that they have behaved immorally (i.e., delusions of guilt), but not once their depressed mood has subsided.

On occasions it is not always possible to make a diagnosis of either schizophrenia or manic depression as patients will display both "manic depressive" and "schizophrenic" symptoms (Brockington, Roper, Copas et al., 1991). The concept of "schizoaffective disorder" was developed as far back as 1933 by Kasannin in order to account for those large numbers of people falling in between the two diagnostic groups and also serves to illustrate the shortcomings of a strictly categorical view (Kendell, & Brockington, 1980). The continuum or spectrum view (see Figure 1.1), which has been proposed as an alternative, has at one end unipolar depression, moving through bipolar affective disorder and schizoaffective disorder to typical schizophrenia.

There is now a climate of opinion which argues that such a continuum view may be more appropriate than a simple categorical or bimodal approach (i.e., dividing into a diagnosis of manic depression or schizophrenia). For instance, in the 1970s a study known as the US/UK diagnostic project video-taped interviews with psychiatric patients and submitted them to psychiatrists based in New York and London. One of the predictions, using statistical methods, was that it would be relatively straightforward on the basis of symptoms reported, to put patients into either a schizophrenia diagnostic group or a manic-depressive group. Kendell and Gourlay (1970), on the contrary, found that most people had a mixed picture displaying both types of symptom and therefore not allowing for a clear differentiation between the two groups. Similar findings have been observed in other studies (Brockington et al., 1991; Kendell, & Brockington, 1980). In summary, there appears to be little evidence to suggest that there are any clear-cut natural boundaries between schizophrenia and manic depression. The vast majority of people with an enduring mental illness have a mixture of affective (manic-depressive) and schizophrenic type symptoms. This is inconsistent with Emil Kraepelin's original binary or categorical view of schizophrenia.

## Does schizophrenia exist?

The term "schizophrenia" was originally coined by Eugen Bleuler in 1911. Prior to this Emil Kraepelin, the German psychiatrist, attempted to differentiate between particular types of madness by devising a classification system for serious and severe psychological disorders. Until that point there had been little progress in separating different disorders from one another (Rosenhan, & Seligman, 1988). In this classificatory system Kraepelin assigned a diagnosis of "dementia praecox" (premature deterioration) to individuals displaying particular sets of symptoms. These included inappropriate emotional responses (e.g., "laughing at a funeral"), stereotyped motor behaviour, attention difficulties (e.g., reduced ability to read), sensory experience in the absence of appropriate stimuli (e.g., seeing people when no one was present), and beliefs sustained in spite of overwhelming contradictory evidence (e.g., insisting that one is Napoleon). Later, he proposed subtypes of dementia praecox that still form the basis of subtypes within the concept of schizophrenia today. Although both Kraepelin and Bleuler agreed that schizophrenia was a biological disorder that was likely to recur, they differed with regard to their views about onset and prognosis. Kraepelin believed that the disorder started in adolescence, was incurable, and followed a deteriorating course. Bleuler, the more optimistic of the two, believed that recovery was possible but still overestimated the chronic nature of the disorder.

Many, however, have questioned the entire notion of schizophrenia and some have argued that beyond the minds of psychiatrists, schizophrenia does not exist (Szasz, 1979). Thomas Szasz, the American psychoanalyst and psychiatrist, has contested that not only schizophrenia but the entire concept of mental illness fails to stand up to scientific scrutiny and that it represents nothing more than the medicalisation of madness (Pilgrim, 1990). In his seminal book *The Myth of Mental Illness*, Szasz, like others (Foucault, 1965; Scull, 1979), has argued that psychiatric practice is nothing more than a legitimised form of social control that uses medical terms such as "treatment", "illness", and "diagnosis" to deprive "sufferers" of their liberty. That is, he presents a moral (not necessarily scientific) argument for abandoning the concept of schizophrenia because of its contentious role in depriving people of their personal liberty (i.e., through compulsory incarceration and treatment under mental health legislation). Laing (1967), like Szasz, claimed that it was spurious to "medicalise" patterns of behaviour that could be better understood in social or cultural terms (McKenna, 1997).

From a slightly different perspective, Boyle (1990), unlike Szasz and Laing, recognises that there is such a thing as mental illness. However, she claims that the concept of schizophrenia should be abandoned because mental suffering cannot be reliably and legitimately subclassified into categories and diagnoses such as schizophrenia. This view has also been taken up by Bentall, a clinical psychologist, who has cogently argued that the concept of schizophrenia is neither reliable nor valid, and therefore not clinically and scientifically useful (Bentall, Jackson, & Pilgrim, 1988).

As noted previously, psychiatrists have not always demonstrated consistency with which they have been able to diagnose somebody with schizophrenia and thereby reach the minimum requirements for reliability. In a now famous experiment, Rosenhan (1973) asked a group of people who were free from major psychological symptoms to pretend that they heard a voice to admission doctors at an American psychiatric hospital. These subjects were under strict instruction to behave as they would normally and to be truthful in their answers to all questions apart from those that dealt with auditory hallucinations. They were told to describe the voice as saying "dull", "empty", and "thud". The vast majority of these "pseudo patients" were admitted with a diagnosis of schizophrenia and discharged with a diagnosis of schizophrenia in remission, despite only the presence of a single idiosyncratic symptom.

Although many of the issues of reliability have been addressed by the psychiatric community through the use of operational criteria for different diagnoses (i.e., *DSM-IV*, *ICD-10*, etc.) and the introduction of semi-structured interview schedules that ensure consistency in the type of questions patients are asked (i.e., the Psychiatric State Examination PSE; Bentall, 1990), it is now readily accepted that reliability is a necessary but not a sufficient condition for the validity of the concept (Spitzer, & Fleiss, 1974). The validity of a concept requires further demonstration (Bentall et al., 1988). One recurrent difficulty with the concept of schizophrenia is the poor correlation between symptoms and diagnosis. Many of the symptoms associated with schizophrenia are also found in other disorders. For instance, a third of people diagnosed with manic depression display many of the main symptoms of schizophrenia discussed previously (Goodwin & Jamison, 1992). Delusions are often witnessed in depression (Winters, & Neale, 1983) and hallucinations are found in a wide range of medical and other psychiatric conditions (Bentall, 1990). This, it is argued, undermines the *construct validity* of schizophrenia as it seems to suggest that the boundaries between different diagnostic categories are at best arbitrary (Kendell, 1975). There is good evidence to suggest that many people suffer from symptoms belonging to different forms of psychiatric illness (Foulds, & Bedford, 1975; Sturt, 1981). It has also been argued that the concept of schizophrenia lacks *predictive validity*, the ability of the diagnosis to predict the eventual outcome that can be expected. Although this will be discussed in more detail in Chapter 2, it is now abundantly evident that outcomes from schizophrenia can vary greatly (Castle, Wessely, Van Os, & Murray, 1998; Ciompi, 1980; Thara et al., 1994). The poor predictive ability of the diagnosis is especially evident after the first episode when a significant minority (up to 20%: Shepherd, Watt, Falloon, & Smeeton, 1989) will never experience another episode of schizophrenic symptoms (Kendell, Brockington, & Leff, 1979). Moreover, it is also common for a diagnosis to be altered within the first few years (Fennig, Kovasznay, Rich et al., 1995; McGorry, 1992) and it is therefore unsurprising to find that a diagnosis of schizophrenia does not always allow one to say with any degree of confidence what is the most appropriate form of treatment. For example, not *everybody* who has been diagnosed with schizophrenia will respond to neuroleptic medication (Crow, MacMillan, Johnson, & Johnstone, 1986; see also Chapter 6) although *some* people with affective disorder will (Naylor, & Scott, 1980).

There are clearly problems with the concept of schizophrenia and for such reasons it is perhaps best to view schizophrenia as an abstract concept that helps clinicians and researchers formulate hypotheses and whose validity is ultimately tested by its utility and its ability to predict, explain, and initiate interventions (Birchwood, & Preston, 1991). Bentall et al. (1988) have argued that we should turn our attention away from the syndrome of schizophrenia to study the individual symptoms. There is no doubt that this has been a catalyst for considerable psychological exploration (Chadwick, Birchwood, & Trower, 1996). It should not, however, be a reason to "throw the baby out with the bath water" or to abandon everything to do with the syndrome view of schizophrenia, as this approach has always been productive and useful (as well as flawed).

# Positive and negative symptoms and subtypes of schizophrenia

As a growing number of criticisms are levelled at schizophrenia as a homogeneous and unitary concept, the research for scientifically meaningful subtypes of psychotic disorder has led a number of researchers and clinicians to utilise multivariate statistical techniques such as factor and cluster analysis to identify naturally occurring dimensions or clusters from large data sets taken from patients with a functional psychosis. This approach has been influenced by those who have distinguished between "positive" and "negative" schizophrenia symptoms. Positive symptoms are so called because they are considered an addition to a person's repertoire (e.g., hallucinations, delusions, disordered speech). Conversely, negative symptoms are those that are evident by the blunting of drive and emotion (e.g., social withdrawal, lack of energy, poverty of speech). The main advocates of such an approach have been Andreason in the United States and Crow in the UK.

## Positive symptoms

Schneider (1959) described a set of symptoms which he regarded as pathognomic of schizophrenia. He delineated these particular symptoms, not for any theoretical purpose but because he felt these symptoms were "primary": they cannot be derived from other symptoms. These "first-rank" symptoms can be elaborated or explained in a delusional manner; thus, delusions and hallucinations can be divided according to whether or not they appear to be based on primary phenomena, although in clinical practice the ability to make this distinction is often difficult. The first-rank symptoms seem to fade with time and to be replaced by secondary phenomena (Wing, 1992). In the International Pilot Study of Schizophrenia (WHO, 1973, 1979) there was close correspondence between Schneider's syndrome of positive symptoms and clinical diagnosis given by the doctors in each of the centres throughout this transnational study. "Secondary" delusions of reference and persecution are quite common in mania and severe depression, but usually have religious, subcultural, or bizarre themes and are congruent with mood; thus, an individual with elated mood hearing voices telling him to use special powers to heal would be regarded as mood-congruent (Winokur, Scharfetter, & Angst, 1985).

At the other end of the spectrum of positive symptoms, there is a smaller group of psychotic symptoms characterised by mood-incongruent delusions without other positive symptoms. These may include "monosymptomatic" symptoms, e.g., morbid jealousy, or a belief that an individual gives off an unpleasant smell, and so on. The constellation of related symptoms around a persecutory theme, collectively what we refer to as "paranoid psychosis", includes an encapsulated, internally coherent network of persecutory delusions in the absence of other positive and negative symptoms. Wing (1992) argues strongly that the positive phenomena may be placed into a hierarchy of scarcity–ubiquity in which items higher in the order tend to be associated with items lower down, but not vice versa. As individuals with a psychosis move steadily into relapse (Birchwood et al., 1989) or recover from an acute episode and perhaps continue to display persisting symptoms (Winokur et al., 1985), individuals are, in some sense, ascending and descending a natural hierarchy of positive symptoms.

## Negative symptoms

Negative symptoms primarily concern losses or diminution in emotion, volition, interests (apathy), and sensations of pleasure (anhedonia). Such symptoms are characteristically associated with withdrawal, underactivity, psychomotor poverty, lack of conversation and social contact, and indifference to appearance and safety. Carpenter, Heinrichs, and Wayman (1988) have argued strongly that, within this complex of negative symptoms, a distinction should be made between those that are primary or "deficit" symptoms and those that are secondary or reactive to these or other circumstances ("nondeficit" negative symptoms). Deficits in symptoms refer specifically to those negative symptoms that are present as enduring traits. Secondary negative symptoms are not qualitatively different but are regarded as arising out of depression, drug side-effects or environmental deprivation and may have been transient in the preceding 12 months in an otherwise clinically stable state. Carpenter et al. (1988) show that clinicians can assign patients reliably to these groups; those in their "deficit" group were more likely to be male with poorer premorbid functioning and greater social disability. The ability of clinicians to unequivocally account for negative symptoms as a result of depression, drug side-effects, or environmental deprivation is essential to their criteria and may not always be straightforward in practice, but what the study at least reveals is that in many instances the negative symptoms are not necessarily enduring in terms of both their presence and severity over time.

Based on this positive and negative symptom dichotomy, Andreason (1982) and Crow (1980) have argued that there are two pathological processes in schizophrenia that may occur either separately or together in an individual person. That is, they hypothesise that schizophrenic psychosis could be subdivided into two syndromes: type I and type II. Andreason (1982) has argued that the negative symptom syndrome of schizophrenia (type II) tends to be related to poor adjustment before the onset of schizophrenia, greater cognitive impairment, poor response to treatment, and poor overall prognosis. Subsequently it has been proposed that the underlying cause of this negative symptom syndrome is a brain abnormality particularly associated with enlarged ventricles. In contrast, Andreason hypothesised that the positive symptom syndrome (type I) of schizophrenia tends to be associated with relatively good adjustment before the onset of schizophrenia, a less severe cause, and a good response to treatment. Both Crow and Andreason have argued that positive symptoms of schizophrenia are more likely to be associated with neurochemical as opposed to structural changes in the brain.

Overall, the distinction between positive and negative symptoms of schizophrenia has been helpful. Some people have criticised it on the grounds that it is oversimplistic and not related to findings from multivariate statistical analysis; however, Liddle (1987) examined the pattern of agreement between symptoms in a group of patients at a similar stage in their illness and found that they could be grouped into three not two factors; namely (1) psychomotor poverty (poverty of speech, flat affect, decreased spontaneous movement); (2) disorganisation (disorders of the form of thought, inappropriate affect); and (3) reality disorientation (delusions and hallucinations). This pattern of segregation into three subsyndromes or subtypes has been replicated in a number of other studies using different symptom scales and different statistical techniques (Malla, Ashok, Norman, Williamson, Cortese, & Diaz, 1993).

## Summary

- Schizophrenia is a disorder of thinking characterised by a distortion of reality, and impaired emotion responses, thinking processes, and interpersonal abilities.

- Hallucinations and delusions are considered to be core symptoms of schizophrenia.
- When considering the problems associated with schizophrenia, a distinction can be drawn between intrinsic impairments (e.g., persisting symptoms such as hallucinations) and secondary impairments (e.g., unemployment, loss of confidence).
- Diagnosing schizophrenia has, over the years, proved notoriously difficult, although recently this task has been made easier and more reliable by the use of semi-structured interviews and diagnostic classification systems (i.e., *DSM-IV* and *ICD-10*).
- The increased ability of clinicians to reliably diagnose schizophrenia has not, however, satisfied those who have questioned whether the concept of schizophrenia should exist at all. The diagnosis remains a convention, not a "fact".
- Although it was initially believed that there were two types of schizophrenic symptoms (i.e., positive and negative), recent research has indicated that there may in fact be three (psycho-motor poverty, disorganisation, and reality disorientation).

# Epidemiology, course, and outcome 2

In this chapter we will discuss how many people and which types are affected by schizophrenia. Whether people recover and what influences that recovery will also be touched upon.

Schizophrenia is surprisingly common. The lifetime individual risk is approximately 1% and on average there are 20 new cases per 100,000 population per year. A picture is now emerging that suggests that it is equally distributed across different cultural groups. Yet, the course and outcome for schizophrenia may be influenced by a variety of factors including where a person lives, their gender, socio-economic status, what they were like before they became ill (their premorbid personality), in addition to other biological and psycho-social factors.

## Is recovery from schizophrenia possible?

To a certain extent the answer to this question depends on how one defines and measures recovery. As was pointed out in Chapter 1, Kraepelin originally argued that recovery from schizophrenia was impossible and that people followed an inevitable decline. Many authors (e.g., Warner, 1994), however, take a more realistic but complex view and differentiate between *symptomatic* or *clinical* recovery (defined as remission or loss of positive psychotic symptoms), *complete* recovery (remission or loss of psychotic symptoms plus a return to premorbid levels of functioning), *social* recovery (occupational and social independence), and *psychological* recovery (marked by the absence of adjustment difficulties such as anxiety, depression, hopelessness, and trauma). This latter form of recovery, arguably, is the most difficult to achieve.

Table 2.1 shows the outcome of five recent follow-up studies. Here it is demonstrated (contrary to Kraepelin's assumption) that the

### TABLE 2.1

**Five follow-up studies of people diagnosed with schizophrenia**

| Study | N | Duration of follow-up (years) | First admissions | Dead (suicides) (%) | Clinically recovered (%) | Social recovery (%) | Poor clinical outcome (%) |
|---|---|---|---|---|---|---|---|
| Bleuler (1978) | 208 | 5–20 | 66 | 34(13) | 20 | 51 | 24 |
| Ciompi & Müller (1976/1984) | 1642 | 37 | 100 | 75(?) | 27 | 33 | 18 |
| Huber, Gross & Schuttler (1975) | 758 | 8–28 | 67 | 19(5) | 22 | 75 | 35 |
| Salokangas (1983) | 175 | 7–8 | 100 | 8(?) | 26 | 69 | 24 |
| Sartorius et al. (1986) | 1065 | 5 | 100 | | | | |
|   Developing countries: | | | | 5(2) | 45 | 75 | 29 |
|   Developed countries: | | | | | 25 | 33 | 50 |

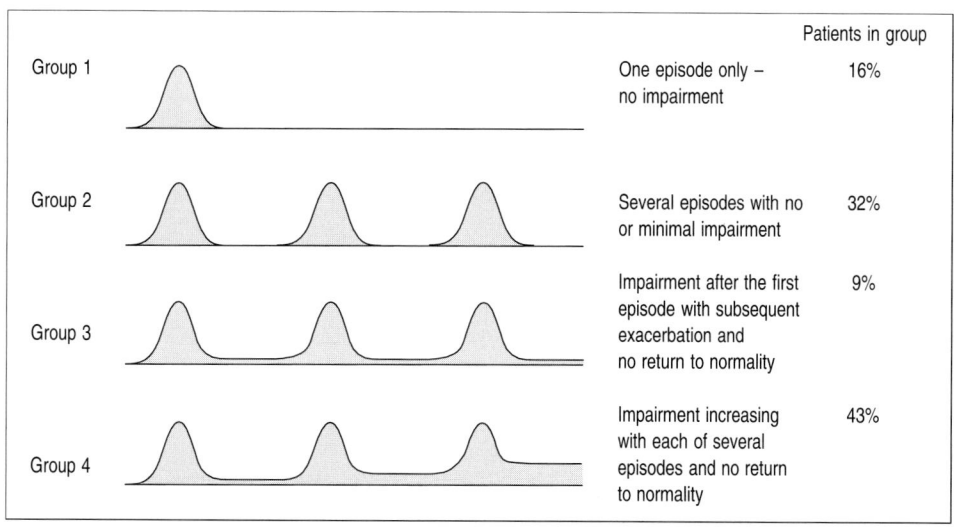

| | | | Patients in group |
| Group 1 | | One episode only –<br>no impairment | 16% |
| Group 2 | | Several episodes with no<br>or minimal impairment | 32% |
| Group 3 | | Impairment after the first<br>episode with subsequent<br>exacerbation and<br>no return to normality | 9% |
| Group 4 | | Impairment increasing<br>with each of several<br>episodes and no return<br>to normality | 43% |

**Figure 2.1.** Heterogeneity of the early course of schizophrenia. From Shepherd, M., Watt, D., Falloon, I.R., & Smeeton, N. (1989b). The natural history of schizophrenia. Psychological Medicine (Monograph Suppl. 16). Cambridge: Cambridge University Press. Reprinted with permission

outcome of schizophrenia is highly variable. Between 20% and 25% will have one episode with full remission, no further episodes and social recovery; on the other hand about 30% will show the poorest outcome. Before reaching any firm conclusion from these studies, a number of points should be borne in mind. First, such studies often overly rely on hospital admission data, which may mean that some people who are not treated in hospital will not be selected. Second, further biasing effects may occur because people with the best outcomes are able to move away and are hard to follow up. Finally, methods of outcome measurement may differ between studies, making it difficult to compare results. With these limitations in mind, a number of observations about outcome from schizophrenia may be made.

The course of schizophrenia is heterogeneous. That is, there is not one but a variety of outcomes. Figure 2.1 shows four patterns derived from a follow-up study of people experiencing an episode of schizophrenia for the first time (Shepherd et al., 1989b). Here it can be seen in that groups 2 and 3 many people experience multiple episodes of psychosis with and without residual symptomatology (symptoms that do not dissipate) and social impairment, respectively. The largest group (group 4) demonstrates how impairment can increase as people experience multiple episodes and relapses. However, it should be noted that there is evidence from earlier (Bleuler, 1978) and more recent studies (Carpenter, & Strauss, 1991) that amongst those who suffer from clinical and social deterioration there may be some relenting of the process and some improvement over time.

## Long-term outcome

Although painstakingly difficult and expensive to carry out, a handful of long-term studies have now charted the course of people diagnosed with schizophrenia over very long time periods. Many of these studies, which have been reviewed elsewhere (Harding, & Keller, 1998; Johnstone, 1991) have followed people for 30 years or more (see Table 2.2).

In this table it can be seen that overall, despite a wide variety of outcomes, there is a trend towards significant improvement and recovery in the majority of patients sampled. This is succinctly illustrated by reference to Courtney Harding's Vermont, USA, study (Harding et al., 1987). Of all the studies, Harding and her colleagues studied the most chronic "back ward" patients, charting their progress over a 32-year period. The study was initially started in the 1950s (Chittick, Brooks, Irons, & Deane, 1961) as part of an evaluation of a combined psychosocial rehabilitation and anti-psychotic medication programme (in the 1950s the phenothiazine drugs were being widely used in the treatment of psychosis for the first time): 269 patients who were considered the most hopeless cases were slowly de-institutionalised and integrated into community support systems. Of the 97% (263) who were located and methodically assessed, 118 patients originally met the criteria for schizophrenia, and 82 of these were still alive 32 years later. As can be seen from Table 2.2, the investigators noted that 62–68% of the sample had completely recovered or shown only mild impairment.

Many have tried to discount Harding's results by reference to the age of the patients involved. The vast majority were older (average age 61) than those in other studies and it has been argued that such a good outcome may be associated with a reduction in dopamine function in the brain that occurs as the normal result of ageing (Breier, Schreiber, Dyer, & Pickar, 1991). Whatever the cause, the findings from the Vermont study and the other long-term studies are

## TABLE 2.2

**Long-term follow-up studies of schizophrenia (from Harding, & Keller, 1998)**

| Investigator | Year of study | Location of study | Number in cohort | Length follow-up (years) | % significantly improved/ recovered | % socially recovered |
|---|---|---|---|---|---|---|
| Bleuler | 1972/1978 | Switzerland | 208 | 23 | 53–68[a] | 46–59[a] |
| Huber et al. | 1975 | Germany | 502 | 22 | 57 | 56 |
| Ciompi, & Müller | 1976/1984 | Switzerland | 289 | 37 | 53 | 57 |
| Tsuang, Woolson, & Fleming | 1979 | Iowa/USA | 186 | 37 | 46 | 21[b] |
| Harding et al. | 1987 | Vermont/USA | 82[c] | 32 | 62–68 | 68 |
| Ogawa et al. | 1987 | Japan | 105 | 24 | 56[d] | 47 |
| DeSisto et al. | 1995 | Maine/USA | 45[c] | 36 | 42 | 49 |

[a] Multiple admissions vs first admissions.
[b] Material status only recorded.
[c] Live interviewed *DSM-III* schizophrenia group—the hardest data.
[d] Derived by adding 33% recovered, with a conservative 23% as significantly improved (from the 46% listed as improved).

suggestive of late recovery in schizophrenia. Certainly the pessimistic views about schizophrenia that prevailed in the early half of the twentieth century appear unwarranted (Zubin, Magaziler, & Heinhauser, 1983).

Outcome from schizophrenia is a complex process and is not simply the result of increasing chronicity of the illness. Strauss and Carpenter (1977) and more recently Harrison, Croudace, Mason, Blazebrook, and Medley (1996) have demonstrated that various measures of social and clinical outcome are only moderately interlinked. For instance, Strauss and Carpenter (1977) found that the severity of the positive symptoms correlated $r = .63$ with the quality and quantity of social contacts, $r = -.49$ with the ability to meet basic needs, $r = -.47$ with employment status, and $r = -.8$ with fullness of life. Likewise, for negative symptoms Wing and Brown (1970) found similar modest relationships between symptoms such as flattened affect and poverty of speech and the level of social functioning. Clearly this suggests that there is not one unitary process but a number of processes influenced by biological, psychological, and social factors.

## Subcultural differences

As far as is known there is no culture or population in the world that is not affected by schizophrenia (Jablensky, 1995). The collaborative study funded by the World Health Organisation (WHO) set out to compare the risk of developing schizophrenia in different countries (WHO, 1979). Using standardised assessment methods, it was demonstrated that the pattern of symptoms shown by psychotic patients in nine countries throughout the world was remarkably similar. On average 1% of the population studied met the stringent diagnostic criteria applied. The lowest rates of 0.5% were found in Aarhus (Denmark), whilst the highest rates were found in rural India (1.7%).

Overall the WHO studies provide evidence that despite showing similar prevalence rates the course and outcome of schizophrenia are more favourable in developing countries such as Nigeria and India than developed nations such as the UK and USA. Other studies are consistent with this view over longer follow-up periods. For instance, a high rate of symptomatic recovery (complete remission of symptoms) of 59% has been reported in Mauritius, 5–12 years after initial onset. This compares with only 34% in London (Murphy, & Rahman, 1971) over a similar period. Likewise, Waxler (1979) noted that 45% of patients admitted for the first time to hospital with schizophrenia in Sri Lanka had not experienced any further episodes and were symptom-free 5 years later. This compares with an average of only 20% in industrialised countries.

A number of possible explanations for such observed differences have been proposed. Although these have been reviewed more thoroughly elsewhere (Jablensky, 1995; Warner, 1994; see also Chapter 4) it is worth considering a few of these in more detail. The idea that differences are spurious because of diagnostic variations between the groups (i.e., Third World countries overdiagnosing milder, better-outcome subtypes of schizophrenia) has largely been dismissed (Jablensky, 1995). In WHO studies outcome was better for all variants of schizophrenia at 2- and 5-year follow-up in the developing countries. Another proposal put forward by Wig, Menon, Bedi et al. (1987) is that families with high expressed emotion, which is evidenced by high rates of critical comments and emotional overinvolvement with the unwell relative and which is a robust predictor of relapse (see Chapter 4), were rarer in Indian than European samples.

Warner (1994) has argued cogently that another possible reason why people from the Third World who develop schizophrenia may do better than their counterparts in more urbanised and industrialised settings in the West is that there are greater opportunities for work and meaningful employment. Warner cites evidence that suggests that in rural, nonwage consistency economies there is no real concept of unemployment and that irrespective of level of functioning there is always a work role for a person with schizophrenia. This is often not the case for people in developed countries where competition for work is common and people are expected to work a minimum of 40 hours per week. As Warner (1994) has written, "industrialised society gives relatively little leeway for adapting a job to the abilities of the worker" (p. 158). The importance of a valid social role for emotional and psychological well-being is well known to both psychologists and sociologists (Champion, & Power, 1995).

Despite this, however, it is unlikely that work alone provides the definitive explanation for differences in recovery rates between developed and developing nations. Beliefs and expectations about mental illness, availability of social support, and stigma in different cultural settings are also likely to be highly influential (Jablensky, 1995). Anthropological studies suggest that in many Third World countries, emphasis is placed on healing and destigmatisation for those demonstrating bizarre behaviours and thoughts (Leff, 1982). Benjamin Paul, the anthropologist who has written extensively about mental illness in rural cultures such as those found in Guatemala, has argued that social resolution and reintegration are essential to the recovery process in such communities. This is in contrast to developing countries where psychotic episodes are likely to lead to increased alienation (Paul, 1967; Warner, 1994). For further discussion of the influence of culture on schizophrenia see Chapter 4.

## Effects of gender

Although a number of early studies found a one-to-one sex ratio in the prevalence of schizophrenia, studies using modern operational criteria have found the incidence of the illness to be higher amongst men than women (Goldstein, 1992). Iacono and Beiser (1992) and Nicole, Lesage, and Lalonde (1992) found an incidence (first episodes) of schizophrenia two to three times higher amongst males than females in two Canadian cities, Vancouver and Quebec. Onset of the illness in males tends to occur on average throughout the world 3½ years earlier than in females (27 years vs 30 years; Hambrecht, Maurer, Hafner, & Sartorius, 1992). There is a further illustration of this in Figure 2.2. This figure shows a large excess of males with onset at 15–30 years and, for females only, a second peak within the range 40–45 years. Thus, the frequency of late-onset schizophrenia was twice as high in females as in males.

Gender also appears to be predictive of outcome from schizophrenia, and this may not be entirely explained by differences in age at onset. Males, on the whole, tend to have higher rates of rehospitalisation, longer hospital stays, and do poorer in community settings (Angermeyer, Goldstein, & Kuhn, 1989). Males may also do worse in terms of showing greater downward drift (i.e., poorer occupational and social functioning; Marneros, Steinmeyer, Deister, Rohde, & Jünemann, 1989). There is some suggestion that females function better socially and do better in the community during both the period prior to the onset of the illness (premorbid period) and what is termed the active phase of schizophrenia (i.e., the first 5 years). Recent studies, however, appear to throw doubt on the idea that superior outcome differences in favour of women can be accounted for solely by their supposedly better premorbid adjustment in the early stages of the illness (Harrison et al., 1996).

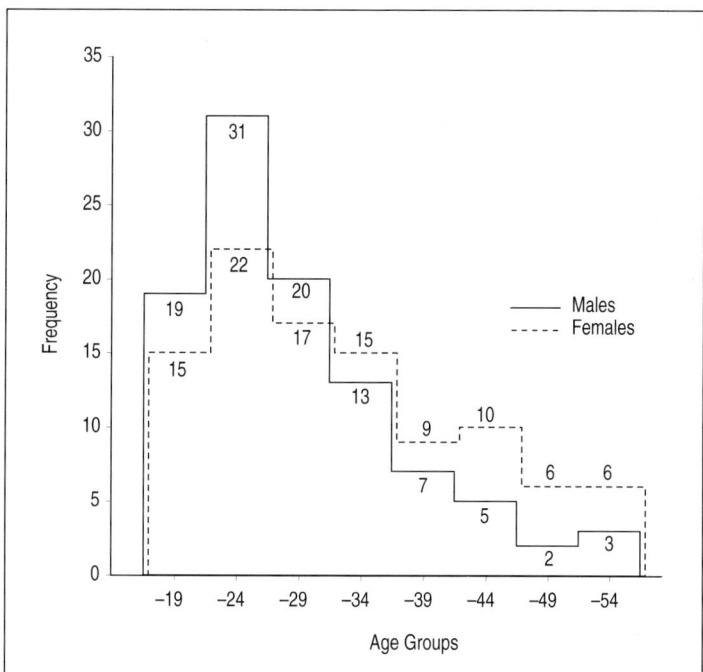

**Figure 2.2.** Gender-specific age distribution in the total sample (WHO-Determinants-Study) (from Hambrecht et al., 1992)

There are a number of potential explanations for the superiority in long-term outcome of females over males. These have been extensively reviewed elsewhere (Haas, & Garratt, 1998). There is, as one would expect, no definitive answer; rather, a number of theories or hypotheses that still need to be fully tested. These vary from the idea that women in general have superior social functioning, not only for schizophrenia, but across all psychiatric disorders, to the theory that such gender differences in schizophrenia are accounted for by the protective function of oestrogen, the female hormone (Seeman, 1982). Another suggestion is that gender differences in social outcomes for schizophrenia can be accounted for by different social roles and social role demands that are placed on men and women in our society. Salokangas (1983), for instance, suggested that although many women with schizophrenia may continue to perform domestic duties and tasks adequately they would be less able to function effectively outside of the home in competitive paid employment. If this is correct, one would assume that, as women begin to take on more and more work traditionally done by men, differences in social outcomes from the disorder would gradually disappear. Again, however, differences in the mean age of onset (which is known to be associated with outcome) may point to the idea that females may have greater opportunities for the achievement of social and developmental milestones before their first episode of psychosis (Haas, & Garratt, 1998).

## Premorbid adjustment

How people function before the onset of schizophrenia has also been shown to be a robust predictor of the outcome and course of schizophrenia. Premorbid adjustment tends to be measured on such factors as a person's ability to establish and maintain friendships and sexual relationships. In addition, performance at school and work tends to decline significantly in those showing poor premorbid adjustment. Often people demonstrating this pattern of adjustment typically report no single identifiable event that triggered the first episode. They tend to report an insidious build-up when symptoms gradually worsen until the psychotic symptoms are apparent. People deemed to have good premorbid adjustment, although they have a greater probability of being hospitalised, have briefer episodes, and a lower rate of future admission (Strauss, & Carpenter, 1972). Premorbid social competence also correlates with lower rates of residual symptoms (2 years after the first episode) and better social recovery including a return to employment (Fenton, & McGlashen, 1987).

There are some suggestions from a recent British study (Harrison et al., 1996), which followed 67 people with schizophrenia over the course of 13 years, that much of the influence of premorbid adjustment on outcome may be accounted for by gender: females demonstrate superior previous social adjustment (Mueser, Bellack, Morrison, & Wade, 1990). There may also be other confounding factors when considering the influence of premorbid adjustment on outcome. Poor premorbid adjustment may lead to greater social isolation, which may in turn influence the rapidity with which people seek help when displaying frank psychotic symptoms. Cole, Leavey, King, Johnson-Sabine, and Hoar (1995) have demonstrated that the presence of a carer when "breaking down" for the first time with schizophrenia is the single most important predictor of whether someone receives help early or late. The duration of untreated psychosis, which averages about 1 year, is a significant correlate of early relapse (Crow et al., 1986) and other short- and medium-term measures of outcome

(Jackson, & Birchwood, 1996). In other words, those with good pre-morbid adjustment are more likely to be living with or in regular contact with a significant other who will help them obtain early treatment and reduce their untreated psychosis.

## Social and familial support

It is now generally assumed that the social environment to which a person with schizophrenia is exposed during and following remission of acute symptoms has a significant impact upon recovery and outcome. Much is now known about familial influences on recovery and the long-term outcome of schizophrenia (Barrowclough & Tarrier, 1992; see Chapter 4).

In contrast, relatively few studies have demonstrated how non-familial social support influences the recovery process. This is despite the findings from the WHO studies (WHO, 1979) demonstrating a positive link between the role of social relationships and the course of schizophrenia (Randolph, 1998). The most notable exception to this is a study by Erickson, Beiser, Iacono, Fleming, and Lin (1989) who followed up, over a period of 18 months, people in one of three groups: first episode schizophrenia, first episode affective psychosis, and a control group comprising a sample of community volunteers matched on gender and age. Ratings of both the quantity and quality of people's social networks and resources were made with the use of the Interview Schedule for Social Interactions (ISSI; Henderson, Byrne, & Duncan-Jones, 1981). People with schizophrenia reported fewer friends and less close and confiding relationships than the other two groups. After 18 months it was found that greater involve-ment with nonfamily members and reports of higher quality social relationships were associated with better prognosis in those with schizophrenia. This association was reversed, however, when con-sidering family members. That is, there was a tendency for those with the greatest number of family members in their social network to report the poorest outcomes. Although this study is not without fault (e.g., 31% refused to take part) it clearly illustrates the importance of good quality social relationships outside the family for people with schizophrenia. Although it is still extremely difficult to disentangle cause and effect (i.e., does poor prognosis lead to poorer social relationships or do poor social relationships impact upon recovery and outcome?), there does appear to be a growing case for attempting to improve the quality of the social networks of people with schizophrenia (Thornicroft, & Breakey, 1991; see Chapter 7).

## Symptoms and subtypes of schizophrenia

The presence of negative symptoms in the early stages of schizophrenia is predictive of poorer early and late outcome (Beiser, Fleming, Iacono, & Lin, 1988; Thara et al., 1994). For instance, the international pilot study of schizophrenia (WHO, 1979) noted that flatness of affect, social withdrawal, and "personality change", coupled with an insidious onset, all predicted poor outcome 2 and 5 years later (Sartorius, Jablensky, Ernberg, Leff, Korten, & Gulbinat, 1997). Negative symptoms, which are thought to be the cause of much social disability and handicap may also place great strain and burden upon relatives and are often a source of confusion within the family (Smith, Birchwood, Cochrane, & George, 1993). Lack of activity, conversation, or emotion is often attributed to the patient rather than the illness (Barrowclough, & Tarrier, 1992), which may in turn lead to overtly critical comments, high expressed emotion, and relapse (Leff et al., 1982; see Chapter 4). In contrast, some have argued (e.g., Andreason, 1982) that schizophrenia with a predominance of positive symptoms (voices and delusions) and acute onset tends to be associated with good adjustment prior to the onset of the first episode and a good response to treatment (see Chapter 1).

## Comorbidity: Depression and suicide

Schizophrenia may give rise to other specific psychological and psyhiatric problems. Depression, suicide, social anxiety, and drug misuse (the so-called comorbidities) may have a significant impact upon the course and outcome of the disorder (Jackson, & Iqbal, 2000; Linszen, Dingemans, & Lenior, 1994; Siris, 1995). This is particularly the case for depression and suicide, which are believed to be very common amongst people with schizophrenia. Although the prevalence of depression in psychosis is difficult to ascertain exactly (estimates range from 22% to 75%, depending on the criteria used), estimates of suicide rates remain alarmingly high and stable at around 10–15% for those diagnosed with schizophrenia (Birchwood, & Iqbal, 1998; Roy, 1986).

The presence of affective symptoms (depression) has long been held to be associated with favourable outcome (McGlashen, 1988).

However, this view is beginning to change. Depression and suicidal thinking is often the cause of crisis and readmission (Shepherd et al., 1989) and has been shown to be predictive of later relapse (Johnson, 1981) and suicide (Roy, 1986). The Northwick Park Study (Johnstone, Crow, Johnson, & MacMillan, 1986) found that subjective feelings of depression and hoplessness at first admission predicted earlier first readmission; on the other hand, presence of depressive delusions (i.e., suggestive of an affective psychosis) were associated with *better* early outcome.

There may be a number of reasons why people become depressed before, during, and after an episode of psychosis; these have been reviewed in more detail elsewhere (Birchwood, Iqbal et al., 2000; Jackson, & Iqbal, 2000; Siris, 1995). One argument that has emerged is that depression following a psychotic illness may be an individual reaction to the changes associated with the psychosis itself. Individuals experience a radical change in their personal lifestyles and commonly express feelings of alienation and loss of self-esteem. Roy, Thompson, and Kennedy (1983) suggest that patients with negative symptoms are at greater risk as these can cause difficulties for the patient on commencing his or her lifestyle, and may also lead to further undesirable life events. Barnes, Curson, Liddle, and Patel (1989) observed that subjective experiences of deficits in chronic schizophrenia, in areas such as thinking, feeling, and perception, were associated with vulnerability to depression. Comparisons of schizophrenics who have and have not developed depression suggest that the nature of the experience of psychosis is a major factor in the onset of depression (Chintalapudi, Kulhara, & Avestri, 1993). Depressed subjects were found to have had a significantly longer duration of the acute psychotic phase, better premorbid adjustment (i.e., good social and sexual adjustment prior to the onset of psychosis), and an excess of stressful life events. Similarly, results from Birchwood, Mason, MacMillan, and Healy (1993) show that depression following acute psychosis may be viewed as a psychological response (demoralisation) to an apparently uncontrollable life event (the psychosis) and all its attendant disabilities.

## Summary

- Schizophrenia is a relatively common and severe psychological disorder that will affect in the course of their lives approximately 1 in 100 people.

- Despite early pessimism, recent well-designed longitudinal studies have indicated that approximately two-thirds of people diagnosed with schizophrenia will make a substantial recovery.
- The course and outcome for schizophrenia will be determined by a number of biological, psychological, and social factors.
- In general, women and people from developing countries will have more favourable outcomes than men and those from developed countries.
- What someone was like before they became ill (premorbid adjustment) may be a significant predictor of how well that person will recover from schizophrenia.
- Good social support and the absence of negative symptoms and post-psychotic depression will also help aid recovery.
- A significant number of people with schizophrenia (approximately 1 in 10) will kill themselves.

# Biological aspects 3

The most striking feature of research in schizophrenia over the last 20 years has been the rise of biological models that seek to explain the symptoms as a manifestation of disturbed brain processes. There is no single biological model, much as there is no single psychological approach. Rather, a number of biological approaches have been pursued from genetics, to anatomy, through to the neurochemistry of the brain. In this chapter we explore each of these approaches in turn and return to the central question—is schizophrenia a biological disorder?

## Is schizophrenia inherited?

The genetic hypothesis of schizophrenia has its origins in early observations that schizophrenia tends to run in families and that the risk for schizophrenia among relatives of an affected individual increases as a function of familial (genetic) relatedness. The first systematic family study was published by Rüdin (1916), who found that what was then known as dementia praecox was more common among the siblings of people with schizophrenia than the general population; this was followed by a large study of over 1000 individuals by Kallman (1938), which showed that both siblings and offspring had increased rates of the disorder. These earlier studies were recognised as flawed since it was not possible to determine whether the cases were representative of schizophrenia as a whole as the diagnostic criteria used were unclear; also, many of the siblings and relatives who were studied had not completely passed through the maximum period of risk (i.e., 18–35 years), thus potentially underestimating the true level of risk; in other words, the risk statistics needed to be age-corrected. Gottesman and Shields (1982) brought together the results of these earlier studies, which are presented in Table 3.1. It will be recalled that since the risk for

| | TABLE 3.1 | | |
|---|---|---|---|

**Lifetime expectancy (morbid risk) of schizophrenia in the relatives of schizophrenics (from Gottesman, & Shields, 1982)**

| Type of relative | Lifetime expectancy (%) | $r^*$ |
|---|---|---|
| **First degree** | | |
| Parent | 5.6 | 0.30 |
| Siblings | 10.1 | 0.48 |
| Siblings with one parent schizophrenic | | |
| Children | 12.9 | 0.50 |
| Children with both parents schizophrenic | 46.3 | 0.85 |
| **Second degree** | | |
| Half siblings | 4.2 | 0.24 |
| Uncles/aunts | 2.4 | 0.14 |
| Nephews/nieces | 3.0 | 0.18 |
| Grandchildren | 3.7 | 0.22 |
| **Third degree** | | |
| First cousins | 2.4 | 0.14 |

\* Correlation in liability assuming general population morbid risk of 1%.

schizophrenia in the general population is generally thought to be in the region of 1%, the data must be compared with this baseline figure. These data indicate that the risk to siblings and offspring is in the order of 10%. The table shows that where the relation is one of *first degree*, the risk is substantially higher than those where the relationship is one of *second degree* (uncles, aunts, nephews, and nieces).

The more recent family studies have used standardised methods of assessment and modern operational criteria for schizophrenia and have been careful to choose more appropriate samples and assess relatives blind to the diagnosis of the individual in question. The importance of operational criteria and well-selected controls is suggested by the study of Kendler and Gruenberg (1984); they assembled a sample of 253 *DSM-III* defined cases of schizophrenia and reported a lifetime risk of 3.7% among first-degree relatives compared with a lifetime risk in normal controls of only 0.2%. Importantly, when the criteria were relaxed to include other psychoses within the spectrum, for example paranoid psychosis, the lifetime risk in first-degree relatives of individuals with schizophrenia increased to 8.6%. This was one of the first studies to suggest that if schizophrenia has a biological basis it does not, as it were, "breed true". In general, these methodologically more rigorous family studies find a range of lifetime risk in the first-degree relatives ranging from 3% to 17% (Gershon, De Lisi, Hamovit, Nurnberger, Maxwell, & Schreiber, 1988). We may conclude that the narrower the criteria for schizophrenia, the lower the risk in first-degree relatives; the broader the criteria, the higher the risk. This underlines the now prevalent view that whatever is genetically predisposed it is not "true" schizophrenia but a disposition to a spectrum of psychosis.

There is usually a strict distinction made between affective and nonaffective psychoses in familial studies, but Angst, Scharfetter, and Stassen (1983) find evidence for a link between a *continuum* of affective–schizophrenic disorders and a similar continuum among first-degree relatives. As discussed previously in Chapter 1, these data suggest that schizophrenia and affective disorders are not discrete "parcels" of disorder but may form a continuum both phenomenologically and genetically (Crow, 1986).

The family studies have confirmed what is apparent to clinicians, that schizophrenia does tend to cluster within families. These observations have inspired an era of research attempting to unravel the extent to which these linkages are brought about through genetic or environmental influences, or both. Two paradigms have been used to distinguish genetic from environmental contributions: studies of twins and of individuals adopted early in life.

## Twin studies

The assumption here is that for disorders with a genetic component, the concordance rate among monozygotic (MZ) twins (100% of genes in common) where one co-twin has schizophrenia, should be greater than that for dizygotic (DZ) twins (on average 50% of genes in common). Inevitably these experimental paradigms are based on relatively small samples, particularly of monozygotic twins, since of course one would expect only 1% of all MZ twins to be affected by schizophrenia; their conjunction is relatively rare and requires a case inception strategy to cover large populations, usually whole countries. These have usually come from studies conducted in Scandinavia where registers of twins and psychiatric disorder have generally been good, enabling these to be integrated to identify appropriate cases. Table 3.2 shows that the concordance rate for MZ twins (where one twin has schizophrenia) is about three times that for DZ twins. Significantly, although the concordance rate is very high (usually between 40% and 60%), there is substantial *discordance* between MZ twins in the order of 40%. Gottesman and Shields (1982) compute the "heritability" statistic (which in essence reflects a difference between MZ and DZ concordance), arriving at the figure of 66%.

**TABLE 3.2**

Studies of schizophrenia in monozygotic (MZ) and dizygotic (DZ) twins (from Gottesman, & Shields, 1982)

| | Monozygotic | | | Dizygotic | | |
|---|---|---|---|---|---|---|
| | | Proband-wise concordance | | | Proband-wise concordance | |
| Study | No. | (%) | r* | No. | (%) | r* |
| Tienari (1971) | 17 | 35 | 0.78 | 20 | 13 | 0.50 |
| Kringlen (1976) | 55 | 45 | 0.85 | 90 | 15 | 0.56 |
| Fischer (1971) | 21 | 56 | 0.90 | 141 | 27 | 0.70 |
| Pollin et al. (1969) | 95 | 43 | 0.83 | 125 | 9 | 0.41 |
| Gottesman, & Shields (1972) | 22 | | | 33 | | |
| Weighted | | 58 | 0.91 | | 12 | 0.48 |
| Average | | 46 | 0.85 | | 14 | 0.52 |

\* Correlation in liability assuming morbid risk of 1% in general population.

Some of these studies were again open to concerns about the absence of operational diagnostic criteria and prompted a reassessment, applying operational criteria of varying degrees of stringency by Gottesman and Shields (1972). Criteria that focused solely upon a limited range of positive symptoms (Schneider's "first-rank" symptoms; see Chapter 1) gave no evidence of genetic contribution, whereas applying broader criteria based upon *DSM-III*, the estimate of heritability rises to a figure approaching 80% (Farmer, McGuffin, & Gottesman, 1987).

A twin study in Norway (Onstad, Skre, Torgrersen, & Kringlen, 1991) also systematically varied the operational criteria to embrace both schizophrenic and affective disorders, and found that including schizoaffective, atypical psychosis and schizotypal disorders gave rise to greater difference between MZ and DZ concordance rates. However, when Onstad et al. broadened further the range of disorders into the nonpsychotic spectrum, e.g., depression and personality disorder, this greatly increased the *DZ concordance* rate resulting in a reduction in the heritability quotient. These data underline the results of the family studies which suggest that any genetic liability is not linked to a tightly bound definition of schizophrenia but embraces the spectrum of psychotic disorders.

Twin studies from an environmental perspective   The twin study paradigm is a favoured approach for the testing of genetic hypotheses as it represents the only naturalistic means of varying gene dosage under conditions where environmental factors are theoretically held constant. Equally, the paradigm can provide information on the extent of the environmental (i.e., nongenetic) contribution, this being in proportion to the overall *discordance* for schizophrenia between genetically identical twins where one co-twin has developed the disorder. In addition, a comparison of discordant MZ twins might identify environmental variables responsible for the triggering of schizophrenia in genetically vulnerable individuals. Thus, although environmental variables are not directly manipulated (unlike in the adoption studies) the technique is, potentially, highly informative from an environmental point of view.

Doubts have been raised about the validity of the twin study method, which will naturally constrain the earlier prospectus. The strongest criticism has come from environmentalists who argue on the basis of firm empirical evidence from normal twins that MZ twins tend to be managed in a similar fashion by their parents (in comparison with DZ twins) and tend to have the same friends (Lytton, 1977), thereby invalidating the assumption that environment is held constant. However, the only reason why MZ twins should be treated similarly is because either they are perceived as similar by virtue of their monozygosity or parents respond to pre-existing behavioural similarities in the twins. Regarding the former, studies exist of twins whose zygosity has been misclassified and in these cases behavioural similarities result from *true* zygosity rather than *perceived* zygosity (Scarr, Carter, & Saltzman, 1979). Lytton (1977) has confirmed in an ethological study of 46 normal male twins that similarities in parental management represent *responses* to similar behaviours and that *parent-initiated* behaviours were similar among MZ and DZ twins. Thus the available evidence from normal twin pairs suggests that the rearing environment of MZ twins is more similar than that of DZ pairs but that this is the result of behavioural similarities of MZ twins.

As we have seen, Gottesman and Shields' (1982) presentation of the twin study data, standardising diagnoses across studies, finds the concordance rates average 46% (range 35–58%) for MZ twins and 14% (range 9–27%) for DZ twins, thus clearly highlighting a genetic factor. There is also of course an equally large *dis*cordance in the MZ twins (54%), suggesting that an environmental factor protects against the full expression of the genotype or, alternatively, acts in conjunction with the necessary genotype. It would appear on the surface that nongenetic factors are of equal importance in their contribution to the overall liability to the development of schizophrenia.

There is unfortunately no simple equation between concordance rates and the relative contribution of genetics and environment. The overall population incidence of a disease will have a considerable bearing on the expected MZ concordance rates. Smith (1970) has calculated theoretical concordance rates in relation to the overall heritability of liability and population incidence, on the assumption that genetic and environmental contributions are normally distributed. Thus, if a disease has no heritability, then the MZ co-twin will develop the disease with equal probability to other members of the population (i.e., the concordance rate = population incidence); if the liability is 100% heritable then the concordance rate will be 100%, independent of population incidence. In between these extremes the predictions are surprising. Assuming a lifetime risk for schizophrenia of 1%, if the heritability (see Chapter 4 for definition) is 50% then the predicted MZ concordance rate will be as low as 13%; a heritability of 80% will yield a concordance rate of 37%. The implication is that the observed 46% MZ concordance rate suggests a very major contribution of genotype to the overall liability (see Chapter 4). One further consideration to be borne in mind is that in those twin studies that have reported on the characteristics of the discordant MZ twin, between approximately one-quarter and one-half were diagnosed "schizoid" or evidencing "character/neurotic" disorders. Thus, only 23% were considered "normal". If a broader definition of the psychopathology were adopted, the MZ concordance rate would be even higher.

How then are we to evaluate the significance of environmental factors in the light of these findings? First, of course, the twin study results do support a contribution of environment to the overall liability, amounting to some 20% of the variance. However, estimates of heritability will vary according to the level of environmental variability. With little environmental variation, genetic factors will appear to predominate in individual differences and conversely with greater environmental variability (see Mortonsen et al., 1999). For this reason heritability estimates for IQ derived from twin studies, for example, have been criticised as they do not permit the widest possible variation in environment, thereby spuriously increasing heritability; when relevant environmental variables are allowed to vary (e.g., social class), IQ heritability is significantly affected (Clarke & Clarke, 1974). The same argument might equally apply to twin studies in schizophrenia; that is, the relevant gene dosage is systematically varied, whereas relevant environmental factors are unknown and presumably not varied to their greatest extent. Therefore, studies such as these do not provide an accurate picture of the influence of environment and, in particular, the estimation of a 20% contribution of environment to the overall liability must be considered a minimum figure.

Furthermore, under certain models of the genetic–environmental interaction, a situation can be conceived where the environmental influence might outweigh other factors. If it is assumed that normally distributed genetic and environmental factors operate additively in some way to achieve a threshold of liability for the expression of the schizophrenia phenotype, then it is plausible that a subgroup of schizophrenics exists whose liability principally comprises the environmental pathogen. Support for this possibility comes from studies of perinatal complications and season of birth in schizophrenia, which are reviewed later in this chapter.

In summary, the twin studies unequivocally point to a major genetic contribution; however, they point also to an essential environmental component, which could well be underestimated and in some cases outweigh genetic factors.

## Adoption studies

Adoption studies have sought further to clarify the respective contribution of genes and environment as this approach more clearly separates them than the twin method. The typical strategy is to identify offspring of individuals who later develop schizophrenia but who are adopted away within days or weeks of birth. Thus, they share no genes in common with their adoptive family, conveniently separating the genotype from the effect of being reared by someone with schizophrenia. The first adoption study was reported by Heston (1966) studying the adopted-away offspring of 47 mothers with schizophrenia and comparing them with a control group matched for age and sex who were adopted soon after birth by mothers who were psychiatrically well. Heston diagnosed the offspring without knowing the parental diagnosis and found that 16% developed schizophrenia (i.e., 16 times greater than chance).

These early findings were followed up with considerable sophistication, combining the registers of adoption and of psychiatric disorder available in Denmark; these studies have come to be known as the Danish-American Adoption Studies. These have employed one of two paradigms. The work of Rosenthal and colleagues (1968) used a similar approach to Heston, whereas Kety et al. (1976) used the so-called "Adoptees Family Study" design where the probands are individuals adopted away early in life who subsequently develop schizophrenia, but the focus revolves around the risk for psychosis in their biological and adoptive parents.

The initial report from Rosenthal found that 3 offspring of 47 parents with schizophrenia themselves developed schizophrenia compared with none of the offspring of the 47 matched controls; when the case definition was extended to include "schizophrenia spectrum disorder" the offspring had a higher risk (18.8%) than the adopted-away children of controls (10.7%). A reanalysis of these data using *DSM-III* criteria by Lowing, Mirsky, and Pereira (1983) found a low rate of schizophrenia in the adopted-away offspring (1 out of 39) but a much higher rate when broader spectrum disorders are included (schizotypal personality disorder and schizoid personality). This research confirmed earlier evidence that what is inherited is a spectrum disorder ranging from mild to severe psychosis and adds support to the continuum theory. This research group also identified 28 children with no family history of disorder who were reared ("cross-fostered") by parents later developing schizophrenia (Wender, Rosenthal, Kety, Schulsinger, & Weiner, 1974); the cross-fostered group did not show an elevated level of psychosis, suggesting that parenting by someone with schizophrenia is not a risk factor. It is of interest that the rate of schizophrenia in the normal control group was still higher than one would have expected, suggesting that the process of adoption, or alternatively the reasons for adoption, are connected with raised risk for schizophrenia.

The adoptees family design of Kety et al. finds an increased incidence of schizophrenia and related disorders in the biological relatives of adoptees with schizophrenia (20.3%) compared with that of control relatives (5.8%). Again, the Kety data have been re-examined (Kendler, & Gruenberg, 1984) using *DSM-III* schizophrenia and schizotypal personality disorder as the case definition. It was found that 13.3% of 105 biological relatives of adopted-away cases were affected, compared with only 1.3% of 224 control adoptive parents. An adoptive study conducted by Tienari, Wynne, and Moring et al. (1994) extended the adoption paradigm to include direct measures of the quality of the adoptive environment. They found that lifetime risk in the adopted-away offspring of parents with schizophrenia was 9.4% compared with 12% in the control group, but reported that the disorder was only expressed in the context of the families rated as disturbed. This provides support for the model outlined by Birchwood, Hallet, and Preston (1988), which argues that vulnerability to schizophrenia may be raised or lowered according to the status of interactions between the individuals and familial or other influences (see Chapter 4, Figure 4.1).

The adoption studies have suggested that the rate of schizophrenia among the high-risk offspring does not vary in spite of profound changes in the rearing environment. However, they have served to clarify that what is inherited is a disposition to a range of psychiatric disorders, rather than a "pure strain", and that ultimately the expression of the genotype depends upon complex interactions at an intrauterine and psychosocial level.

## Modes of transmission

If there is a genetic risk for schizophrenia, it follows from the foregoing review that any pattern of inheritance is complex and irregular and that the clustering of schizophrenia within families cannot be modelled according to simple Mendelian principles. A further way of reconciling complex patterns of inheritance with Mendel's laws derives from attempts to understand the genetic basis for continuously varying characteristics such as height and IQ. This has led to the notion of polygenic or multifactorial inheritance, which models complex traits arising from the conjoint operation of a number of different genes, together with an interaction with environmental agents. This continuum model can still have relevance to characteristics (like schizophrenia) that are present or absent by invoking the concept of *liability*. Liability to the disorder is assumed to be distributed continuously in a population, but the model holds that only when this liability exceeds a particular threshold is the phenotype disorder manifest. These models assume that genes and environmental factors act in an additive way so that the overall liability is normally distributed in the population. Genetic models have advanced considerably in recent years with the growth of the discipline of molecular genetics, which is a rapidly expanding field encompassing an ability to map the complete human genome.

# Molecular genetics

The major application of molecular genetics has come with the large-scale so-called "linkage" studies of families who show a clustering of schizophrenia within and between generations. The assumption here is that such clustering might reflect the impact of a single gene. Linkage analysis is a method of finding gene loci (markers) that are sufficiently close on a chromosome, leading them to be inherited together with the disease from one generation to the next. In such cases the marker and disease are said to be linked. The distance between supposed illness genes and the locus of the marker can be calculated by observing the number of recombinations during meiosis; the closer the disease locus is to the marker the less likely recombination is to occur.

One approach to this is the study of Mendelian "subforms" of disorders, which has been used successfully in Alzheimer's disease, noninsulin-dependent diabetes, and breast cancer. In spite of the fact that several research groups have conducted a large-scale search for linkages, no clear-cut replicated forms have yet been found (Cloninger, 1994). However, given the possibility that there may be more than one major locus that can cause schizophrenia, the best hope for this approach lies in the use of data sets, gathered from a very large number of families. Initially, linkage studies concentrated on chromosome 5. Sherrington, Brynjolfsson, Petursson et al. (1988) studied five Icelandic and two British families with schizophrenia emerging over at least three successive generations in at least two family members. They found a high concordance for linkage to chromosome 5, which was obtained only for the broadest definition of psychiatric disorder. However, further studies (e.g., McGuffin, Sargeant, Hetti, Tidmarsh, Whatley, & Marchbanks, 1990), have failed to demonstrate a chromosome 5 linkage. Further evidence for a susceptibility locus for chromosome 11 also received some support in some but not all studies (e.g., Wang, Black, Andreasen, & Crowe, 1993). As Owen and McGuffin (1991) point out, although these families are multiply affected with schizophrenia this does not necessarily indicate the operation of a single major gene. Moreover, clustering can occur even under conditions of polygenic transmission.

Two further strategies are now prominent in the molecular genetic field. *Allele-sharing* methods attempt to show that the pattern of markers from a particular chromosomal area is *not* consistent with random Mendelian segregation. This is done by attempting to demonstrate that pairs of relatives affected with schizophrenia inherit identical copies of a particular region on the chromosome more often than expected by chance. In *association studies* the frequencies of different alleles of a marker are studied in groups of patients with the disorder and controls, with the aim being to detect an association between a particular allele of the marker and the presence or absence of disorder. These associations reveal susceptibility loci only when the marker is itself close to the susceptibility locus and need to be conducted therefore using markers very close to, or indeed within, candidate genes. One problem of this approach is that the studies can end up as "fishing expeditions" as there is no clear basis on which to choose one gene over another.

These kinds of linkage analyses have not resulted in consistent findings and more recent large-scale collaborative investigations are underway to compensate for the problems inherent in studying a disorder that is both heterogeneous and for which no universally accepted definition exists. The linkage methodology is best suited to the testing of single gene hypotheses and, given the likelihood that any genetic vulnerability to schizophrenia may be the result of multiple genes, it is a high-risk research strategy.

# Childhood precursors of schizophrenia

One way of studying supposed genetic influences is to observe behavioural anomolies *before* the manifestation of the phenotype (psychotic symptoms). Thus, the children who are at risk of developing schizophrenia and, retrospectively, the early years of people with a definitive diagnosis, have come under scrutiny.

It has long been understood that many individuals who develop schizophrenia manifest psychological and social difficulty long before the onset of the positive psychotic symptoms. Systematic studies of the childhood functioning of people with schizophrenia have shown that changes occur in between one-half and two-thirds of individuals who later develop the disorder, and that subtle, and not so subtle, behavioural and social impairments may be observed on average between 2 and 3 years prior to the first psychotic episode (Beiser, Erickson, Fleming, & Iacono, 1993). The observation that such difficulties may stretch back to early adolescence and even childhood has inspired *developmental* theories of schizophrenia but has also raised questions about whether it is possible to predict *who* will later develop schizophrenia and whether there are any biological, psychological, or social markers associated with the raised risk, thus providing valuable clues to understanding the causes of schizophrenia.

## High-risk studies

Over 20 *high-risk* studies have now been reported in the literature. It is a research strategy that developed in the 1950s and 1960s with the aim of following through children whose higher genetic risk is confirmed through their having at least one parent with schizophrenia. This is an important strategy because it enables individuals to be studied in depth, blind to their eventual outcome. One of the many problems with research of this nature is that it is indeed "high risk" in that it can only begin to provide answers once individuals are through the period of high risk, i.e., once they reach their 30s, by which time scientific and technical advances may have occurred and rendered the research obsolete.

Fish, Marcus, Hans, Auerbach, and Perdue (1992) report an irregular pattern of early motor development, and in mid-childhood find a similar difficulty in fine motor control and co-ordination. Difficulties in attention and information processing have been widely reported (e.g., Erlenmeyer-Kimling, 1987) with social and cognitive deficits becoming more pronounced in later childhood and adolescence as individuals approach the high-risk period. For example, Worland, Weeks, Janes, and Strock (1984) report a decline in IQ scores, particularly in verbal function.

Examining school reports and teachers' observations during adolescence is a favourite strategy and one that consistently reveals a pattern of difficulty in emotional development, for example being easily upset, inappropriate behaviour in class, and particular difficulties in forming and maintaining relationships. The Israeli High Risk Study (Ingraham, Kugelmass, Frenkel, Nathan, & Mirsky, 1995) found that the single most powerful predictor in mid-adolescence was a poor "locus of control", which is an index of a lack of agency or sense of control over events, particularly in the social domain. Responsibility for good outcomes is characteristically attributed externally and the individual may feel an observer of events, rather than one who can participate or assume control over them. This pattern is linked to low self-esteem. One major drawback of the high-risk paradigm is again the difficulty of distinguishing between genetic and other effects that emerge as a result of being reared in a family where one or both parents have schizophrenia. The Finnish adoption study of Tienari, Wynne, Moring, Lahti, et al. (1994) shows that the presence of disturbance in the adoptive families increases the risk for later schizophrenia but only in those children whose biological parents had schizophrenia. This implies an interaction between psychosocial and genetic risk factors and the developing vulnerability to schizophrenia. Recent advances in the technology of brain imaging (see later) are being brought to bear upon the possibility of subtle brain abnormality in individuals with higher risk of schizophrenia. For example, Sharma, du Boulay, Lewis, Sigmunds-son, Gurling, and Murray (1997) showed that individuals at risk for schizophrenia have an increased frequency of neuroradiological abnormalities, particularly enlargement of brain ventricles; and an imaging study by Keshavan, Montrose, Pierri et al. (1997) suggested neuroanatomical abnormalities of the medial temporal cortex.

## Retrospective studies

These studies investigate precursors of adult-onset schizophrenia by examining medical or school records of individuals with a known diagnosis in adulthood. The main advantage of this is that a representative sample of the patient population is obtained, not simply those with one or more parents with schizophrenia; one drawback of this method, however, is that where information is derived from relatives or patients themselves, it suffers from recall bias. As indicated in the previous section, during adolescence a growing difficulty in the interpersonal and intellectual domains is generally observed, which is particularly strong in males. An ingenious approach to this was the study conducted by Walker and Lewine (1990) who obtained a sample of old home movies collected from families of schizophrenic patients who were less than 8 years old at the time of filming, and compared these with a control group, which included their well siblings. Subtle but significant neuromotor abnormalities were documented when compared with their unaffected siblings; neutral observers were also able to distinguish those who later developed schizophrenia at a level much greater than chance. These provocative findings support the notion that there are subtle problems in the maturation of motor systems in the early childhood of many individuals later developing schizophrenia. This was confirmed by Hollis (1995) in a sample of patients of adolescent onset (less than 17 years) who showed that they had much higher rates of developmental impairments in language, motor, and social functions affecting up to one-third of cases.

## Birth cohort studies

One of the best approaches to the investigation of developmental disorder as a precursor of schizophrenia is the longitudinal studies of general population samples. In the UK two birth cohorts of the normal population were obtained, in 1946 (Jones, Rodgers, Murray, &

Marmot, 1994) and in 1958 (Done et al., 1991), and followed up 20–30 years later, so that they had all lived through the maximum period of risk. Jones et al. investigated a sample of approximately 5000 individuals, some 30 of whom were given a definite diagnosis of schizophrenia. These individuals had a significantly later onset of walking (by an average 6 weeks) and were three times more likely to have had speech and language problems in childhood and adolescence. The cases also had poorer educational attainments at ages 8, 11, and 15 and were more than twice as likely as controls to show solitary play preference at ages 4 and 6. By age 13 they rated themselves as less socially confident. At 15 years, teachers rated them as less sociable and more anxious than controls. These results were not gender-linked. The mothers of these children were almost six times more likely than mothers of controls to have manifested difficulties in parenting skills and in understanding their child, which can of course be construed as both cause and/or effect of early developmental difficulty.

The study of Done, Johnston, Frith, Golding, Shepherd, and Crow (1991) identified 40 cases from the 1958 birth cohort with a subsequent diagnosis of schizophrenia, 35 with affective psychosis and 70 with neurotic disorders. At age 7 the "preschizophrenic" males were more likely to be rated by their teachers as engaging in inconsequential behaviour, showing anxiety for acceptance and hostility. At age 11 the males remained much the same, while the "preschizophrenic" girls were more likely to show increasing social withdrawal than difficult behaviour. These data were interpreted by Done et al. as suggesting that preschizophrenic boys were somewhat more socially inappropriate and had difficulty grasping social conventions, whereas the girls showed increasing signs of social withdrawal.

## Neurodevelopmental theories

Over the last decade or so the emerging data on the childhood precursors of schizophrenia have crystallised in the form of a general neurodevelopmental framework. This argues that the origins of schizophrenia, or more probably of a subgroup of the spectrum, lie in abnormalities of the developing brain during foetal and perinatal life. Weinberger (1987) is credited with the germ of this theory, arguing that a brain lesion arising during foetal development gives rise to subtle cognitive and behavioural manifestations in childhood. Later as the brain develops its higher cortical functions this produces abnormalities, particularly in the verbal domain as indicated by the quintessentially verbal nature of many psychotic symptoms including the auditory hallucinations and delusional thinking. Two sources of evidence are marshalled in support of this model: (1) evidence suggesting that individuals with schizophrenia have experienced a higher rate of brain insult during pregnancy, and (2) evidence from the study of gender differences in schizophrenia which suggests that males in particular are susceptible to neurodevelopmental abnormalities.

There is considerable evidence that pregnancy and birth complications are detrimental to the health of the developing foetus. Several studies of perinatal and birth complications (PBCs) in schizophrenia have been conducted, some of which have relied on maternal recall and others of which have examined birth records directly. The majority of these studies have indeed supported an association between the presence of PBCs and schizophrenia. The PBCs have included low birth weight, premature births, "small for date", prolonged labour, hypoxia, and foetal distress (O'Callaghan, Gibson, & Colohan, 1992). Not all studies have reported positive findings: The birth cohort study of Done et al. (1991) discussed earlier failed to find any difference, although their measures of PBCs were rather unconventional. A number of studies have suggested that PBCs are particularly associated with schizophrenia of severe rather than mild type (O'Callaghan et al., 1992), early onset, and of *lower* genetic risk (Lewis, & Murray, 1987).

In order to examine whether those patients with PBCs showed evidence of brain insult, studies have used modern imaging techniques. A review of the salient studies reveals an inconsistent picture, with nine studies supporting an association between the presence of PBCs and indices of brain damage such as enlarged ventricles (e.g., Owen, Lewis, & Murray, 1988), whereas eight further studies find no relationship or an inverse one. These are fascinating developments, but they have not yet been adequately tested using the greater resolution of recent scanning technology such as magnetic resonance imaging (MRI).

One of the most consistently replicated findings is the excess of late winter births in people with schizophrenia and a relatively lower number born in the summer and autumn (see Torrey, Bowler, Taylor, & Gottesman, 1990). This reliable phenomenon accounts for an excess in the order of 10–15%. The Danish high-risk study (Machón et al., 1983) found winter births were associated with inner city residence, i.e., raising the question of exposure to seasonal viruses. Subsequent investigations have suggested that foetal exposure to influenza, particularly during the epidemic of 1957, raised the risk for schizophrenia. A number of studies have examined this hypothesis to determine whether there is indeed an excess of individuals born in the UK during 1957 with a diagnosis of schizophrenia. Many positive links have been reported (e.g., Mednick, Machón, Huttunen, & Bonnett, 1988) and in some studies epidemics over several decades have been studied showing an excess of schizophrenic births in each one (e.g., Sham, O'Callaghan, Takei, Murray, Hare, & Murray, 1992). It is possible that it is not exposure per se that mediates this effect but mothers' immune response to the virus; Wright, Murray, Donaldson, and Underhill (1993), for example, have suggested that some mothers produce an anti-influenza antibody which crosses the blood–brain barrier of the foetus, and causes subtle damage to the developing brain.

As previously discussed in Chapter 2, there has been growing interest in the gender differences within the schizophrenic spectrum. Castle, Scott, Wessely, and Murray (1993) reported data from a first episode sample. Here, schizophrenia was most common in males, but least common in older males (>25 years). Those whose first illnesses manifested before the age of 25 were predominantly male, single, had poor work and social adjustment, and showed signs of a premorbid personality disorder. This has been linked to evidence that males with high PBCs are associated with a younger age of onset (O'Callaghan et al., 1992) and poorer outcome (Alvir et al., 1999). It is the poorer outcome for males, their earlier onset, evidence of neurodevelopmental abnormality in the context of lower genetic risk (Goldstein, Faraone, Chen, & Tsuang, 1992), and poorer response to medication (Liberman et al., 1993), which have together led to the theory that males are particularly prone to a severe form of illness consequent upon neurodevelopmental illness (Castle, & Murray, 1991).

What are we to make of these diverse sources of evidence about the childhood precursors of schizophrenia? It seems clear that in many ways the onset of positive psychotic symptoms represents the "end of the beginning" of the development of schizophrenia, particularly for males. The data are persuasive that during childhood and adolescence a majority of individuals with schizophrenia display clear evidence of emotional and psychosocial difficulty, possibly linked with subtle brain abnormality. Normal child development is understood as arising from complex transactions between genetic, neurodevelopmental, and psychosocial influences. Rutter and Sroufe (2000) argue for a dynamic approach to "developmental psychopathology", stressing an interplay between intrinsic and extrinsic factors; the liability for schizophrenia may vary over the course of development as genetic and environmental factors continue to interact across the continuum of liability. The notion of a liability is, as we have seen, consistent with the genetic studies and also with the evidence from the study of schizotypy in normal populations (Claridge, 1997); see also Chapter 5.

Neurotransmitters    Genetic factors will exert their influence through the "hardware" of the brain. In the remainder of this chapter we consider what is known about brain anomalies from the function of the individual brain cell through to the major structure of the brain.

The brain is a neurochemical structure of many millions of neurones which make up the main anatomical structures of the brain, including the lobes of the surface of the brain or cortex, the midbrain structures including the thalamus, hypothalamus and the limbic system, and the structures of the brain stem. A number of important observations encourage the view that it is at the neuronal level that the hypothesised biological basis of schizophrenia is played out. First, the efficacy of some of the neuroleptic drugs used to control the positive symptoms have a particular affinity for certain kinds of neurones and point to a role in the causal pathway. There are also many "street drugs" that are known to mimic psychosis, for example the hallucinogens such as LSD and amphetamine can exacerbate psychotic symptomatology in those already vulnerable. Recently the genetic evidence itself and the latest advances in molecular genetics together are helping to unravel complex relationships between brain chemistry and the human genome.

Neurones are arranged in a number of different circuits employing different chemicals or neurotransmitters. These include the monoamines, the amino acid neurotransmitters and the neuropeptides. Early investigation of neurotransmitter mechanisms used both indirect methods, for example the presence of metabolites in urine and the blood, and direct methods through examination of post mortem brain tissue. Recently *in vivo* methods have been permitted following advances in neuroimaging. The monoamines which have been the focus of research in schizophrenia include dopamine, noradrenaline and serotonin (5-HT). The activity of these neurotransmitters and that of the enzyme responsible for their metabolism, monoamine oxidase (MAO), has been examined.

Dopamine is the most widely researched of the neurotransmitters and it maintains a central role in biochemical theories. For over three decades the "dopamine hypothesis" of schizophrenia proposed that there is excessive dopaminergic activity in the brain indicating some kind of aberration of this neurocircuitry. The dopamine theory arose because of evidence that amphetamines and other drugs that have an impact on the dopaminergic system can induce a state that mimics psychotic symptoms in otherwise healthy individuals (e.g., Harris, & Bakti, 2000) and can exacerbate psychotic symptoms among those who are vulnerable. Second, the neuroleptic drugs, which are effective in managing psychotic symptoms, have in common the function of blockading dopaminergic neurones (Johnstone, Crow, Frith, Carney, & Price, 1978). However, attempts to assess directly the supposed excess presence of dopamine in the brain have proved equivocal. For example, investigations of the presence of a metabolite of dopamine, homovanillic acid (HVA), have produced no evidence that it is present in cerebral fluids to a greater extent than in normals (e.g., Sumiyoshi, Hasegawa, Jayathilake, et al., 1990). Studies of post mortem brains have similarly failed to provide clear and consistent evidence for increased dopamine turnover in the brains of people with schizophrenia.

It was later suggested that there may not be increased dopamine turnover but rather the receptors may be particularly sensitive to dopamine; this led to investigations of the capacity of the different neuroleptic drugs to bind with different classes of dopamine receptors with different sensitivities (these came to be known as D1 or D2 dopamine receptors). Data from post mortem studies suggest that the D2 receptor in particular is present in abundance in the brains of people with schizophrenia and that many neuroleptic drugs seem to have a particular affinity for the D2 but not the D1 receptors (Cross, Crow, Killpack et al., 1978). What is not clear, however, is whether the increased proliferation of the D2 receptor in the schizophrenic brain, which is now well established, is the result of the use of neuroleptic medication itself and unrelated to any primary pathology.

The new brain imaging techniques such as positron emission tomography (PET) and single photon emission computed tomography (SPECT) have been used to assess neurotransmitter receptors in living humans and have been used to clarify the continued uncertainty about the status of the D2 receptors in schizophrenia. Studies including Pearlson, Tune, Wong et al. (1993) and report major increases in D2 receptors in patients not previously exposed to neuroleptics. Recent advances in molecular biology have unravelled up to five receptor subtypes (D1–D5) and pioneering work by

Seeman et al. (1993) using PET found a six-fold elevation of the density of the D4 receptor in schizoprenia (D4 has close similarities in gene structures and pharmacological profile to the D2 receptor).

## Noradrenaline

Wise and Stein (1973) suggested that negative symptoms in particular might be affected by a deficit in noradrenaline, which has been implicated in the "reward system" or pleasure centres of the brain. Although later attempts to examine the activity of noradrenergic systems did not find a reduction in brain samples of people with schizophrenia (Wyatt, Schwartz, Erdelyi, & Barchas, 1975), subsequent studies have suggested that chronic long-term neuroleptic treatment can itself reduce noradrenergic activity (Cross et al., 1978).

## Serotonin

The serotonin hypothesis is usually credited to Wooley and Shaw (1954), who argued that there might be a specific serotonergic dysfunction on the basis of a structural similarity of drugs, particularly LSD, to the serotonin molecule. Once again studies of the metabolites of serotonin have not confirmed these speculations (e.g., see Potkin, Weinberger, Linnoila, & Wyatt, 1983) and attempts to increases serotonin activity through provision of oral doses of its precursor have failed to produce improvements in schizophrenic symptoms (e.g., Gillin, Kaplan, & Wyatt, 1976).

Once again the growth of molecular biology has identified subtypes of the serotonin receptor and studies have reported a significant reduction in 5HT-2 receptors in the prefrontal cortex (Laruelle, Abi-Dargham, Gasanova et al., 1993). These findings have been tied in with the dopaminergic theory by Ohouha, Hyde, and Kleinman (1993), who argued that serotonergic underactivity in the prefrontal cortex leads to failure of inhibition of activity in the subcortex, leading in turn to increased dopaminergic activity.

## Amino acid neurotransmitters

Gamma amniobutyric acid (GABA) is one of the major inhibitory neurotransmitters in the brain, which are known to interact with dopamine systems particularly in the limbic system; thus a notion of an interlinked deficiency in GABA and hyperactivity of dopaminergic systems has been an attractive hypothesis. Again studies from post mortem data have not proved consistent (Perry, Kish, Buchanan, & Hansen, 1979) and, overall, biochemical evidence does not support any role for GABA deficiency in the brains of people with schizophrenia. It therefore is not surprising that attempts to test a GABA agonist have proved negative as a treatment for positive symptoms (Tamminga, Crayton, & Chase, 1978).

Glutamate is an excitatory neurotransmitter particularly found in cortical neurones. These systems have attracted particular interest because they link systems within the cortex with projections from the midbrain including the lymbic system. This is of interest since it has been argued that schizophrenia may be linked to a failure of *integration* of cortical function between the key functional areas of the brain including the hemispheres.

Overall there is no agreement that glutamatergic systems are altered in the brains of schizophrenics. Since interest in glutamatergic neurones has been at the level of connectivity between cortical pathways, focus has not been upon the elucidation of simple deficits or excesses of this neurotransmitter. For example, studies have suggested that areas around the temporal lobe including the limbic system show deficits in glutamatergic activity (e.g., Deakin, Slater, Simpson et al., 1989), whereas in the prefrontal areas of the cortex there appears to be overactivity. Further work by Deakin, Slater, Simpson, and Royston (1990) suggests that these deficits in the temporal lobe arose as a result of atrophy of brain tissue lateralised to the left side.

## What is the status of the neurochemistry of schizophrenia?

There is overwhelming evidence that the major antipsychotic drugs have in common an ability to block dopamine receptors; but it is also clear that the hypothesis of dopaminergic hyperactivity as the principal cause of schizophrenia is an oversimplification. Schizophrenia as we have described it throughout this book is a heterogeneous collection of symptoms and subtypes, and these characteristics have not properly entered into research for neurotransmitter aberration in schizophrenia. It is also clear that the neurotransmitter systems interact and that cortical pathways are only beginning now to be mapped. Such interactions have focused on the neurotransmitters of the tempero-frontal cortex which is particularly significant in view of the results arising from *in vivo* imaging studies suggesting abnormal activation of these areas of the brain, an area to which we now turn.

# Neuroanatomy

The search for abnormalities in key anatomical structures of the brain has a long history. It was Emil Kraepelin himself who argued that a degenerative process underlies what he believed to be an essentially deteriorating disorder. This remains one of the major research strategies in the search for a biological basis for schizophrenia. Typically this strategy involves comparing people with schizophrenia and controls on measures such as the volume and size of anatomical structures, cell counts, and hemispheric differences in structure indicative of abnormal lateralisation of brain function. Investigation of post mortem brains is a favoured strategy; as we have seen, however, this is not without its problems, for example the impact of acquired neurological or vascular disease, which is more apparent in people with schizophrenia, and the impact of lifelong use of neuroleptics, can confound the results. The arrival of modern scanning techniques, particularly computerised tomography (CT) and magnetic resonance imaging (MRI), have enabled high quality resolution of images of brain structures to be obtained among living subjects. It is also true that just about every structure in the brain has been implicated at some point as abnormal in people with schizophrenia, though recent scanning data do point to consistent changes in some areas of the brain.

## Brain size and weight

A key question is whether any neuropathological changes are localised in particular brain regions or are part of a whole-brain process. There has been much attention to this issue. Studies of post mortem brains have revealed mixed findings. Although some indicate a decrease in brain weight by up to 10%, other studies find no difference in brain weight and volume between schizophrenics and controls (Falkai, & Bogerts, 1995). The CT and MRI studies have by and large failed to find differences in either whole-brain or cortical volumes; thus, if there are major changes to brain structure these must be focal and not diffuse.

## The limbic system

The limbic system is a subcortical structure including the hippocampus, amygdala, and cingulate gyrus. The system is thought to have a role in the regulation of emotion and has projections into the temporal areas of the cortex. Many such investigations have been undertaken of post mortem brains and subtle but significant cell loss in one or more of these structures has been observed, which the imaging studies confirm (e.g., Jernigan, Zisook, Heaton et al., 1991), always with evidence of unusual cell connectivity in the hippocampus.

## Midbrain structures

Cell loss and diminished volume of tissue in thalamic structures have been reported (Bogerts, 1989). Changes in the volume of the basal ganglia have also been noted although evidence suggests that these may be a consequence of chronic neuroleptic treatment (Chakos, Mayerhoff, Loebel, Alvir, & Lieberman, 1993). Studies of the brain stem have found no abnormality in cell numbers in the key structures of the brain stem, including the substantia nigra and the locus coeruleus.

## Cortex and corpus callosum

The corpus callosum has attracted particular interest in the light of powerful evidence for the presence of abnormal lateralisation and interhemispheric communication (Flor-Henry, 1983). The corpus callosum is a large bundle of fibres providing the main cortical connection between the hemispheres. There are consistent reports of gender differences in thickening of these fibres in normals that are reversed in schizophrenia (Nasrallah, Olson, McCalley-Whitters, Chapman, & Jacoby, 1986). Volumetric measures of overall cortical volume including grey matter have shown virtually identical values for schizophrenics and normals (Heckers, Heinsen, Heinsen, & Beckman, 1991).

## Evidence for abnormal early brain development

Three stages in the development of the cerebral cortex are now understood. This essentially consists of growth of so-called precursor cells, which migrate into an intermediate zone of the brain before "sprouting'; and then proceeding towards the surface of the cortex and finally settling in the cortex proper. At this point the development of neuronal dendrites and organisation of the synapses takes place. There has been considerable research examining the "architecture" of cortical structures suggesting that a disorder of the final stage of brain development occurs in many people with schizophrenia, involving the final migration of neurones in the cerebral cortex. Cellular disarray in the structures of the limbic system and temporal lobe are thought to be consistent with the late migration and differentiation of neurones that takes place in the second and third trimesters of pregnancy (Falkai, & Bogerts, 1995).

It is known that in normal humans the two hemispheres subserve different functions and that structurally they are not mirror images of one another. This asymmetry is particularly marked in the temperoparietal region of the cortex. Two structures including the sylvian fissure and planum temporale are usually longer and larger in the left compared with the right hemisphere. Studies by Falkai and Bogerts (1992) showed that there is a considerable reduction in this asymmetry of these structures, particularly in males with schizophrenia. Data from scanning studies show broadly similar findings; for example, Szeszko, Bilder, Wu et al. (1995) were unable to find the usual structural asymmetries in the prefrontal regions of the cortex.

# Functional brain imaging

The past two decades have seen an explosion of studies of cerebral function in addition to those of structure through brain imaging. Advances in positron emission tomography (PET) and single photon emission computed tomography (SPECT) have permitted examination of the functional structure of the living brain. Growth changes in brain structure may be determined using X-ray computerised tomography (CT) or magnetic resonance imaging (MRI). In order to link localised disorders of brain function with particular symptoms of schizophrenia, functional imaging such as PET and SPECT is used to generate images of regional brain activity. Finally, as we have already seen, it is also possible to determine images of the molecular components of brain tissue, particularly the neurone receptors for which PET or SPECT scans are employed.

## Structure

The fluid carrying cavities of the brain (ventricles) have been shown to be enlarged, which is direct evidence of reduced brain tissue or atrophy. Johnstone, Crow, Frith, Husband, and Kreel (1976) were the first to report such enlargement using CT methodology in a chronic schizophrenic sample. A large number of studies comparing ventricular volume with controls have been undertaken and a meta-analysis of these is reported by Raz and Raz (1990). Over half the studies report a significant increase in ventricular size and the meta-analysis attempted to determine the size of the difference in relation to the overall variation of patients and control samples; this is known as the *effect size* and they quote a value of 0.6 standard deviations which, although a significant finding, implies that the size of the effect is small and requires large samples to obtain sufficient statistical power. However, as we have seen in relation to abnormalities of early brain development, the presence of a modest effect may be linked to major anomalies of brain function.

As noted earlier, the application of scanning methodologies, particularly the MRI scans, to whole brain tissue have suggested reductions in tissue volume particularly in the temporo-frontal areas consistent with abnormal lateralisation.

A study of monozygotic twin pairs discordant for schizophrenia by Reveley, Reveley, Clifford, and Murray (1982) found that the affected twin had a larger ventricular brain ratio (VBR) in 6 out of the 7 pairs. A subsequent study by Suddath, Christison, Torrey et al. (1990) found that in 14 out of 15 cases the affected co-twin had a smaller bilateral hippocampus volume than the nonaffected twin. They also monitored ventricular volume and found that the affected twin had larger ventricles, consistent with the assumption that large ventricular sizes are associated with diminished brain tissue. This is a very powerful observation. When the genotype is controlled for, discordance is linked to diminished brain volume. The fronto-temporal areas are closely linked to language and the organisation of behaviour: this echoes strongly the study by Boklage (1977) who examined the correlation between concordance for handedness and schizophrenia using the British sample of Gottesman and Shields (1972). He found that in the 12 pairs concordant for right handedness, 11 were concordant for schizophrenia. Of the 16 pairs not concordant for right handedness only 4 were concordant for schizophrenia. This would suggest that abnormal localisation arising from a brain anomaly affects the schizophrenic co-twin.

Significantly, where scans have been repeated several years after the initial scan the results are usually replicated, for example the presence of enlarged ventricles; but these abnormalities did not reveal a worsening with time, suggesting that in most cases this is not part of a degenerative pathology (e.g., Vita, Sacchetti, & Cazullo,

1988). There have been many attempts to link these structural changes with the presence of particular symptoms. One obvious candidate for association with ventricular enlargement is the negative symptoms, but the results of 18 such studies do not provide strong support for this link (Lewis, 1990).

## Function

When the brain is engaged in different information processing or motor tasks, the imaging techniques are able to detect an infusion of blood to the relevant parts of the cortex, indicating that regional cerebral blood flow (CBF) is an index of localised brain activity. It has thus become a favoured strategy to examine brain function. The usual technique involves introducing an isotope into the bloodstream, which is positron emitting and which can be picked up using the PET technique. Monitoring the brain of people with schizophrenia in a resting state has produced in many studies evidence of *under*activity of the tempero-frontal areas of the cortex, a phenomenon that has come to be known as "hypofrontality". The earlier studies showed conflicting results but there does seem to be a consensus that hypofrontality is more prevalent in chronic patients (Liddle, 1996). The methodology has now developed into two paradigms, one involving measuring CBF in patients in whom the symptom of interest is present and comparing it with those for whom it is absent. The other involves selectively engaging different parts of the brain through use of an information processing task and comparing patients and controls in the activation of the area of interest.

With regards to the former, two breakthrough studies have been reported. First, McGuire, Shah, and Murray (1993) studied CBF in association with the activation of auditory hallucinations and found a link with increased blood flow to Broca's area in the left temporal cortex.

In Chapter 1 we described the dimensional approach to psychosis, championed by Liddle. These dimensions include reality distortion (hallucinations and delusions), disorganisation (formal thought disorder), psychomotor poverty (poverty of speech, flat affect), and psychomotor excitation (pressure of speech, lability of affect, and depression). In 1992, Liddle, Friston, Frith et al. used PET in the study of patients with stable symptoms who were receiving neuroleptic medication. They found that psychomotor poverty was associated with increased CBF in the prefrontal cortex and left parietal cortex, and disorganisation with decreased CBF in the right prefrontal cortex, while reality distortion was associated with increased CBF in the left temporal lobe. These observations have been replicated (e.g., Suzuki, Yuasa, Minabi, Murata, & Kurachi, 1993).

In a landmark study by Weinberger, Berman, and Zec (1986), it was observed that CBF among individuals engaged in the Wisconsin Card Sorting Test (WCST; which demands cognitive flexibility to promote problem solving) is closely associated with damage to the frontal and prefrontal lobes of the brain. Weinberger et al. confirmed that schizophrenic patients not only performed poorly on this test, as others have found, but that during performance there was a lowered blood flow in the prefrontal cortex. There was in other words a strong correlation between the level of CBF and performance on this cognitive task. A study of discordant monozygotic twins by Berman, Torrey, Daniel et al. (1992) has found evidence of reduced frontal activity during this task in the affected twin, once again supporting the notion that at least in the case of monozygotic twins the discordance may arise as a result of subtle brain (frontal) impairments linked to early trauma or abnormal neurodevelopment.

A study by Andreasen, Rezai, Alliger et al. (1992) involved patients who had not received neuroleptic medication performing the "Tower of London" task, which requires strategic planning implicating the frontal lobes. This revealed a reduced activation of the prefrontal cortex, suggesting that the effects noted by Weinberger were not an artefact of medication. Finally in an ingenious study by Liddle et al. (1992) the patient was first given a task involving the simple generation of words which revealed no specific underactivity of the frontal lobes; whereas in more complex tasks requiring co-ordination of activity between the frontal and temporal lobes hypo-activity was noted, suggesting that hypofrontality is linked with abnormal co-ordination between these key centres of the brain.

## Summary

- The evidence for a biological component in the aetiology of schizophrenia is strong. It is clear that such contribution occurs across a spectrum of psychosis, not "schizophrenia" per se.
- For many, changes occur before the onset of the positive symptoms and a variety of brain mechanisms are involved.
- None of these proposed mechanisms however are sufficiently well understood and their status can be best described as "risk factors".

- There are a number of environmental risk factors (e.g., inner city residence), which, when considered as a population basis, can outweigh genetic risk.
- Conceptually it is parsimonious to think of biological factors, particularly genetic risk, obstetric risk, or developmental deviance, as contributing towards individuals' *liability* to develop psychosis.

# Stress–vulnerability models  4

Studies of the natural course of schizophrenia undertaken prior to the introduction of the neuroleptic drugs reveal a very variable pattern: in particular, the capacity of many patients' acute symptoms to remit and then to return as it were "spontaneously", was regarded as part of the natural progression of the illness (Bleuler, 1978). Thus even while individuals remained symptom-free, they clearly revealed a propensity to manifest further symptoms; in other words they remained *vulnerable*. The factors governing the transition from vulnerability to psychotic state continue to fascinate the schizophrenia researcher.

A seminal study conducted over 30 years ago raised the possibility that psychosocial stress could trigger the reappearance of symptoms in vulnerable persons. The British social psychiatrists Wing and Bennett (Wing, Bennett, & Denham, 1964), showed that in the course of attempting to rehabilitate long-stay residents of psychiatric hospitals by training them in "industrial" tasks, many began to manifest psychotic symptoms after many years of stability. At around the same time, reports began to appear suggesting that persons living with families were at greater risk of relapse (Brown, 1959; Brown, Monck, Carstairs, & Wing, 1962) than those returning to live in other settings, for example those living alone.

These early findings encouraged the view that psychosocial stress generated by stressful life events, including those arising from disordered family life, could trigger or exacerbate psychotic symptoms in vulnerable individuals. This idea was articulated with considerable clarity by Joseph Zubin (Zubin, & Spring, 1977), who presented his "stress vulnerability" model of schizophrenia. This model argues that an underlying vulnerability to the illness can be activated to produce psychotic symptoms dependent upon the severity of psychosocial stress and the strength of the underlying vulnerability; thus those with a high vulnerability will require little in the way of social stress to trigger symptoms, whereas those with a lesser vulnerability will require greater levels of stress to trigger the psychosis.

The "social reactivity" of schizophrenia now forms part of the classical teaching of psychiatry and in this chapter we examine the principal sources of evidence for this assertion: the studies of life events, family life, cultural and ethnic differences, and broader socio-economic factors.

# Life events and schizophrenia

## Early retrospective studies

The now classical study of Brown and Birley (1968) documented the number of life events preceding a recent episode of psychosis and found that approximately 50% of people experience at least one major life event in the 3 weeks prior to relapse, which represented a significant increase over the preceding 9 weeks in which only 12% experienced a life event. By contrast, a large community control sample reported a low and unchanging level of life events in the same period. The concentration of life events within a brief period suggested that life events triggered a relapse. This remains a highly influential study and a number of subsequent investigators, using broadly similar methodology, have found support for Brown and Birley's initial findings.

Jacobs and Myers (1976), using a standard inventory (The Social Readjustment Rating Scale: Holmes, & Rahe, 1967), failed to find an excess of life events in the 12 months prior to the first episode in a sample of 62 schizophrenic patients compared with a sample of normal controls. This does not contradict Brown and Birley's data since they found an excess of events in the 3 *weeks* prior to onset, which would be masked by the 12-month inclusion period. Hardesty, Falloon, and Shirin (1985) measured life events in 217 first admission psychiatric patients of whom 35 had a diagnosis of schizophrenia, using the same methodology as Jacobs and Myers. They too found no excess of events in the year prior to onset and there was no relationship between number of events and the severity of symptoms, although there was a concentration of events in time of 12 weeks prior to relapse.

Birley and Brown (1970) argued that life events would be more likely to trigger relapse in those who received neuroleptic medication for psychosis. If someone is going to relapse while on medication it will require a potent life event to trigger this (whereas those not on medication would require little or no life stress to trigger a relapse). Leff et al. (1973), in the context of a trial of neuroleptic medication comparing an active with a placebo drug, found the rate of life events in the drug-relapsed group to be 44% vs 22% for the placebo-relapsed group. Leff et al. concluded that medication could be viewed as possessing a stress-buffering function.

## Methodological development

The possibility that life stress could precipitate psychotic episodes has been intensively researched since these pioneering studies, but conclusions are difficult to draw as the studies have not always been explicit about the possible functions of life stress and how it impacts on psychosis. The following possibilities should be clearly distinguished:

1. Schizophrenia arises as a specific consequence of severe stress associated with life events or crisis *without* the presence of any underlying vulnerability.
2. The timing of schizophrenia, the first or subsequent episodes, is influenced by the experience of life events. Thus, the *probability* of the first or of other episodes developing is determined by other factors.
3. The probability of an episode is influenced by the experience of stressful life events.

It is also important to bear in mind that the subjective level of stress may vary as a function of the number or severity of life events and individual differences in vulnerability to the impact of life stress. With regard to the first of our possibilities, it must be demonstrated that people with schizophrenia experience more stress than other psychiatric or normal groups. In fact, when the period immediately prior to onset is examined, people suffering from depression experience substantially more stressful life changes than those with a diagnosis of schizophrenia (Jacobs, & Myers, 1976). Indeed all the studies of life events rarely find that more than 50% of patients experience more than one life event in the period immediately preceding a psychotic relapse. Thus, it is most unlikely that schizophrenia represents a specific response to stress without evoking the presence of a specific vulnerability.

In order to test these hypotheses, a number of methodological difficulties need to be overcome which were endemic in these early retrospective designs (Day, 1989; Malla, & Norman, 1994). The main difficulty is that inherent in all retrospective studies: how many patients face similar life events *without incurring an emergence of symptoms*? By focusing only on those individuals who have relapsed, the dice are loaded in favour of the hypothesis. What is required is to measure the timing and severity of life events independently and then to determine the probability of a subsequent relapse in relation to those events. This will require a truly prospective design. A second problem concerns the issue of retrospective bias. It is possible that informants asked about their perceptions of the timing and severity of life changes may, in a desire to rationalise their illness, distort the timing of the event to "explain" the relapse. Ideally, therefore, the measure of life events needs to be ascertained to a degree independently of the individual experiencing them.

There is another difficulty. Many of these early studies used control groups but it is not clear what the appropriate control group is for a group of people with schizophrenia. As Bebbington, Wilkins, Jones et al. (1993) indicate the nature of their illness may affect the rate of life events they experience. For example, one might expect a lower frequency of life events because the illness might lead to withdrawal from certain aspects of life that might otherwise provide a rich source of life events (e.g., social relationships). Thus, it is not clear what advantages the use of a control group bring to this area and there is now general agreement that the clearest evidence in support of the triggering role for life events in psychotic relapse comes from a design when the patient is used as his or her own control; in other words finding a peak of events in the weeks preceding the psychotic episode. It is also possible as we have indicated that people with schizophrenia may be abnormally sensitive to the impact of stress and it is difficult to establish an appropriate control group with similar sensitivities. This is, then, another reason why using the patient as his or her own control is the most appropriate design.

There are two further methodological issues that have bedevilled this area of work, which concern the personal meaning or significance of life events. The break-up of a marriage or the death of a relative may be distressing for some but a relief for others; there is a need to ascertain the "contextual threat" and to acknowledge the personal significance or stressfulness of the life changes. Of course, asking the patient to rate the stressfulness or contextual threat of a life event immediately raises the problem that individuals may seek to rationalise a relapse by subjectively increasing the perceived potency of a life event.

One approach to this dilemma has been pioneered by Brown and Harris (1978) in relation to depression; this involves the elicitation of life events and difficulties using a standardised schedule (LEDS: Life Events and Difficulties Scale) and then a panel of independent raters attributes a severity rating to the event, taking account of the individual circumstances. This method is a compromise between problems of retrospective basis whilst ensuring some weight is given to the individual and context. Brown and Harris (1978) also considered the problem of the extent to which life events are truly independent of the illness or are possibly linked to it; for example, the break-up of a marriage might conceivably be the *result* of problems and difficulties associated with caring for someone with schizophrenia. Brown and Harris introduced the innovation of classifying life events into those that are *independent*, *possibly independent*, and *dependent* on the illness in question.

## Second generation studies

The next wave of studies sought to take account of these methodological difficulties in varying degrees. Most notably, in a multi-centre World Health Organisation study Day et al. (1987) used a retrospective design similar to that of Brown and Birley but were careful to distinguish independent from dependent events, and to determine the presence of life events *first* before ascertaining the presence or absence of a psychotic relapse. They found that those experiencing a psychotic relapse showed an elevation of independent life events in the 12 weeks before relapse which replicated in five out of six centres across the world, providing striking support for Brown and Birley's original findings.

Bebbington and colleagues (1993) in the course of a broader study of psychosis identified 51 individuals as having a psychotic relapse within the preceding year. This group used the LEDS procedure 6 months prior to the relapse, compared with a psychologically healthy group living in the same locality. They found a significant excess of life events particularly in the 3 months prior to relapse. Chung, Langeluddecke, & Tennant (1986), in a smaller sample, also found an excess of "threatening" events in the 6 months prior to relapse compared with a control group of patients who had not relapsed.

We now turn to the prospective studies. Generally these studies monitor the presence or absence of life changes prospectively over a given time period and determine the overall relationship between the presence of life events and the probability of subsequent relapse. The first study in the USA found no significant changes in positive symptoms in the 3 weeks after a major independent life event had occurred (Hardestey, Falloon, & Shirin, 1985), although this study was limited by the small number of independent life events and the small number of cases (36). Malla, Cortese, Shaw, & Ginsberg (1990) and Ventura, Nuechterlein, and Hardistry (1992) in Canada each reported a 12-month prospective study; whereas Ventura et al. demonstrated an excess of events in the 4 weeks prior to relapse, Malla et al. found no relationship.

Only one study has attempted to bring together the necessary methodological refinements and this was conducted by Hirsch and colleagues (1996) in the UK. This group set out to determine whether and to what degree life events independent of illness increased the risk of relapse and compared those on active medication with those withdrawn from it under experimental conditions. There was also concern to establish whether life events operated proximal to the relapse (4 weeks preceding it) or by acting more cumulatively over a longer period of time, up to 6 months. Seventy-one patients with chronic schizophrenia were followed up for 48 weeks and assessed regularly on the LEDS scale. Half were treated with regular neuroleptic medication while half were recently withdrawn.

The results showed that life events were not clustered in the period immediately preceding relapse but they made a significant *cumulative contribution* over the year of the follow-up period. No interaction between medication status and the ability of life events to trigger an episode of psychosis was found. They found that 23% of the relapse risk could be attributed to life events, and in those with twice the mean rate of events, the risk was 41%. To put it another way, increasing the "dose" of life events increased the risk of relapse. The Hirsch et al. study confirms that life events appear to have some role in raising the probability of relapse as part of a cumulative process but the absence of a cluster of events prior to relapse suggests that they do not "trigger" an episode.

Overall as the methodological sophistication of these studies has developed, the results increasingly point to a role for life events in relapse. The data do not yet unequivocally support the "triggering" hypothesis. It is also difficult to establish whether the life events merely "bring forward" in time the episode of schizophrenia. These debates can only be settled by experimental manipulation, e.g., through a trial of treatment involving the improvement of patients' ability to handle major life events, but as yet, such a study remains to be undertaken.

# Familial influences

Between the 1940s and the 1960s the literature was dominated by the view that schizophrenia arose as a result of deviant socialisation or communication processes within the family. Family theories were prominent in the USA where, under the influence of the psychiatrist Harry Stack Sullivan, the ascendancy of Freudian theory inevitably focused attention on families which were regarded as the pre-eminent influence on psychosexual development.

## Theories of family influence

Early conceptualisations of the role of family life focused exclusively on the mother–child relationship, as developmental theorists viewed this as the most important element in socialisation. A number of clinical observations of these relationships characterised the mothers as cold, overprotective, and domineering. "Schizophrenogenic mothers" were thought to have arrested the development of the child's ego (the sense of self and reality) and that upon encountering the "real world" in adolescence and early adulthood, the demands were such that the adult is forced to escape reality and to retreat into a form of thinking characteristic of early childhood. This form of thought, termed "primary process" thinking is, according to Freud, characterised by narcissism and fantasy, which was felt to bear some relationship to schizophrenic thought processes.

The approach was broadened in the 1950s to include the family as a whole and theories were developed on the assumption that the family should be viewed as a psychosocial system obeying "natural laws". Empirical studies of family life in schizophrenics began therefore to emerge. These more formal theories stemmed from the work of three research groups based in the USA; two of these (Bateson, Jackson, Haley, & Weakland, 1956; Singer, & Wynne, 1963) specifically addressed the nature and style of communication between family members, and the third (Lidz, Hitchkiss, & Greenblatt, 1957) that of family structure and relationships.

Bateson proposed that communication between parents and off-spring was frequently contradictory and placed the child in a "double-bind". This consisted of three components: the first is a "primary negative injunction" prohibiting certain actions; the second, a "secondary negative injunction" conflicted with these prohibitions; and third, a "tertiary negative injunction" indicated that a choice must be made, that there are no means of escape, and that the child is prevented from clarifying the inconsistency. According to Bateson, the inconsistent secondary communication need not conflict at a verbal level; thus the tone of voice, facial expression, or posture with which the primary negative injunction is delivered may be inconsistent with the content of the verbal communication. These incompatible communications were thought to affect the acquisition of an internally coherent construction of reality (or ego development in Freudian terms) and Bateson suggested that patients might thereby generate fallacious constructions such as delusions, and show extreme mistrust of all communications as is sometimes exhibited by paranoid schizophrenics.

Wynne and Singer's theory suggested that parental communication was not inconsistent but rather vague and fragmented, lacking coherence and purpose. According to this theory the child's cognitive and social development is impaired through the absence of a coherent message and a focus of attention which is essential for learning. Wynne and Singer saw a direct relationship between this fragmented communication and the disordered thinking characteristic of many schizophrenics.

The family socialisation theory of Lidz et al. (1957) argues that schizophrenic families fail to provide a cohesive, stable, and supportive environment for the developing child and may fail to provide role-appropriate models. Two abnormal family structures were identified by Lidz et al. "Schismatic" families are those in which the conflicts between parents lead them to compete for the loyalty and affection of family members as a means of undermining the other's influence and control over family affairs. "Skewed" families display abnormal dominance patterns: bizarre and psychopathological behaviour of one marital partner is complemented and supported by the submissive needs of the dominant partner. The children are encouraged to support and acquiesce in the abnormal views of the dominant partner, thereby impairing cognitive and social development. According to Lidz et al., in both kinds of family the divisions between the generations are blurred and parents fail to act in role-appropriate ways. This arouses anxiety about incestuous feelings and schizophrenia is seen as one way of handling the conflicts and distortions of family relationships.

## Implications of adoption studies for family theories of schizophrenia

It is known that schizophrenia tends to run in families over generations. The average risk to a child of a schizophrenic parent is about 14% (vs 1% in the general population) and where both parents are schizophrenic, the risk rises to 46% (Slater, & Cowie, 1971). It is important to note that there will be greater discontinuity over two or more generations and that a majority of schizophrenics do not have schizophrenic parents or siblings. Family theorists argued that these observations were consistent with a familial genesis because the presence of a schizophrenic parent represented an extreme manifestation of disordered family relationships (child rearing, interpersonal relationships, or dominance patterns) responsible for the appearance of schizophrenia.

The demonstration of an inherited component to schizophrenia (see Chapter 3) was not regarded as a refutation of family causation in the early 1960s, because it was considered that a disordered family environment was a necessary condition for the emergence of schizophrenia in genetically vulnerable individuals, and furthermore that in certain extreme cases this could be sufficient on its own (such as being reared by a schizophrenic parent). Indeed, as we have already seen, the discordance in twins suggests an environmental component. Thus, the transmission of schizophrenia within families would arise as a juxtaposition of the inherited genotype and, through rearing by a schizophrenic parent, the negative influence of the family.

One way of testing this special case of the family hypothesis would be to rear the offspring of schizophrenics in a "normal" environment, the prediction being that the incidence of schizophrenia should fall to chance levels or at least to the level found in adopted children generally. A natural form of this ideal experiment can be conceived if a sample of offspring of known schizophrenics adopted away early in life could be traced. Such studies have been undertaken, with major implications for the family theories (see Chapter 3 for a fuller account). Two kinds of adoption methodology have been employed. In the Kety-led studies (Kety, Rosenthal, Wender, Schulsinger, & Jacobsen, 1975), 34 children adopted within a month of birth and later emerging with schizophrenia served as the index cases. Their adoptive and biological relatives' psychiatric status was assessed and compared with a normal (adoptive) control group. The results of these studies were: (1) the adoptive relatives show no elevation of schizophrenia, whereas (2) the biological relatives show a concentration of schizophrenic disorders. These data point strongly to a genetic factor but for present purposes demonstrate that schizophrenia in the rearing family is not a necessary factor in the familial transmission of schizophrenia.

Using a different methodology, Rosenthal and his colleagues assembled a sample of 39 offspring of schizophrenic parents adopted away at an early age. An average of 11 years elapsed between the birth of the 39 adoptees and the first hospitalisation of the index parent. Neither the adoptive families nor the adopting authorities had any knowledge that the biological parent had or could develop schizophrenia. A control sample of adopted children of parents without any history of psychiatric disorder served as the comparison group. Rosenthal, Wender, Kety et al. (1968) discovered 8% incidence of schizophrenia in the index adoptees compared with 0% for the controls. With the inclusion of borderline schizophrenia and subsequent additional cases the figure rose to 18.8% for the index cases (vs 10.1% for controls).

Rosenthal's results, even more so than Kety's, show how difficult it is to break the cycle of schizophrenia from one generation to another through immersion of the genotype in a normal rearing environment. But, as Lidz, Blatt, and Cook (1981) and others have intimated, no measurement has ever been taken of the *adoptive* family environment and they have suggested that there may exist some "schizophrenogenic" influences to account for the high incidence of schizophrenia. However, given the 18.8% incidence of schizophrenia in index adoptive families, this then implies that at least one in five (adoptive) families are sufficiently pathological to trigger schizophrenia. The true figure will need to be much higher as this assumed a most fortuitous pairing of genotype with the pathological family environment. In other words, a pathological rearing environment would need to be so prevalent as to call into question the meaning of the term "pathological" and "schizophrenogenic".

Wender, Rosenthal, Kety, Schulsinger, and Weiner's (1974) remarkable study of 21 adopted children with no family history of psychiatric disorder who were reared by a schizophrenic parent, provides a means of testing whether such rearing is sufficient alone to precipitate schizophrenia. Wender did not find an increased risk for schizophrenia in these adoptive individuals, although it must be pointed out that some parents developed serious psychopathologies other than schizophrenia and did so when the average age of the adopted child was 11 years—past the time when rearing practices might be considered to have had a formative effect.

In summary, the adoption studies have shown that the likelihood of developing schizophrenia in genetically high-risk individuals does not vary in spite of sometimes profound changes in the rearing environment. The adoption technique is naturalistic and prone to bias, for example the incidence of borderline schizophrenia in the normal adoptees is higher than chance, possibly reflecting psychopathology in their (normal) biological parents being partly responsible for their adoption. At the very least the results show that rearing by a schizophrenic parent is not a necessary (and certainly not a sufficient) condition for the emergence of schizophrenia in genetically high-risk individuals. As this form of rearing has to be considered by family theorists as an extreme manifestation of "schizophrenogenic" influences, then the basis for believing that the family in general has an independent role in the aetiology of schizophrenia must be seriously brought into question.

## The family and schizophrenia: A synthesis

The adoption studies have seriously undermined a model of family influence in which the independent occurrence of genotype and family pathology, when juxtaposed, trigger the schizophrenia phenotype. This does not prove that families play no part in the emergence of schizophrenia—much depends on how the role of family life is modelled. The model outlined in Figure 4.1 assumes a unidirectional, continuing influence (a "main-effect" model, see Figure 4.1a). However, families could still exert an effect through a "transactional" process (Figure 4.1b).

Transactional models originate in the child development literature and assume that the child is not a passive recipient of parental behaviour but is an active agent in his or her own development. Samerof and Chandler (1975) invoked a transactional model to explain some child development data which might have a relationship to schizophrenia. Their review demonstrated that disturbances of childhood temperament and cognitive function resulting from parental trauma (e.g., anoxia) can be ameliorated or worsened according to the quality of the "caretaker" (family) environment, in this case as indexed by social class. It was suggested that the families' reaction to or management of these disturbances reciprocally influenced the offspring's behaviour, in turn affecting parental behaviour, and so on. Such transactional influences serve to bring the child toward a homogeneity of developmental outcomes; an extreme of parental disorder and/or poor family adjustment will bring the child

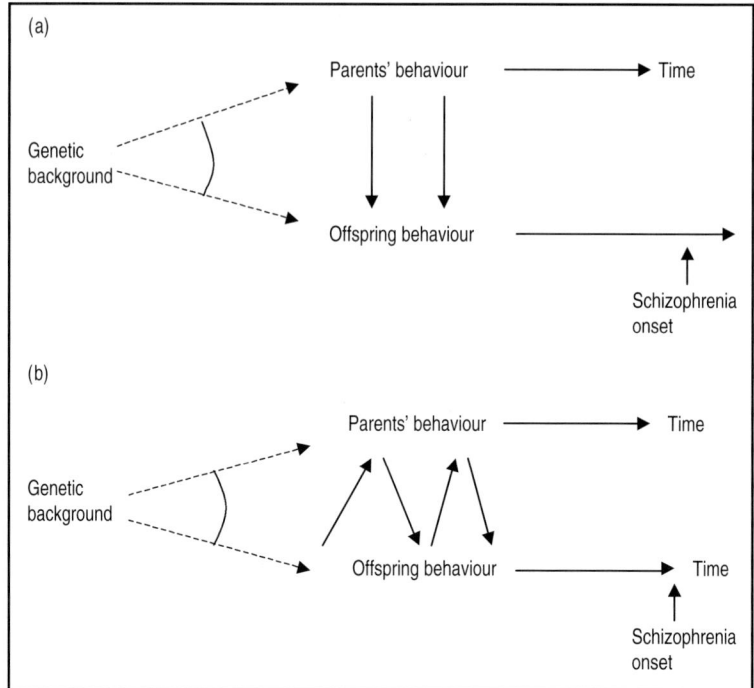

**Figure 4.1.** The (a) "main-effect" and (b) "transactional" family models of schizophrenia

outside these modal outcomes. It is quite feasible that this might operate in schizophrenia because family effects are postulated to emerge as a failure of these long-term transactions to bring the child within "normal" limits.

This specific role which biological *or* adoptive parents may have is that, as a result of a long-term, disturbed transactional processes, the liability to schizophrenia is increased through exacerbation of cognitive, social, and neuropsychological deficits. Additionally, a stressful relationship could develop with the disturbed pre-schizophrenic, thus precipitating the onset.

## Family life and the course of schizophrenia

### The studies of "expressed emotion"

The impetus for this long and successful series of studies was founded on some results reported by Brown, Carstairs, and Topping (1958) showing that people with schizophrenia returning to close relatives (parents or spouses) fared worse than those returning to lodgings in terms of community survival. This study has not since been replicated, although Brown's initial finding that high face-to-face contact between patient and family increased relapse risk does suggest that close relatives may place patients at risk for relapse. This was hypothesised to be relatives' "emotional over-involvement".

Brown et al. (1962) operationalised this in terms of emotion, positive or negative, and hostility rated during the course of a factual interview about the patient. Using a prospective design they found that homes rated high in emotional involvement (a composite of all measures) were strongly associated with clinical deterioration over 12 months. Following methodological refinement to include critical comments rated in terms of tone of voice as well as content (Rutter, & Brown, 1966) a replication was attempted (Brown, Birley, & Wing, 1972). Relatives rated as "high in expressed emotion" (EE), mainly those making more than seven critical comments, were associated with a much higher rate of relapse over 9 months compared with the low EE group (58% vs 16%), statistically independent of the severity of illness. A further successful replication with refinements in measurement by Vaughn and Leff (1976) included a meta-analysis of these two studies ($N = 128$), suggesting that risk factors of high EE, contact time and use of medication, operated in a hierarchical additive fashion such that, for example, patients in low contact (less than 35 hours a week) with a high EE relative and taking medication reduced the relapse rate to 15%, comparable with the low EE group. On the other hand, those in high contact with a high EE relative without medication predicted almost certain relapse (97%).

Subsequently Leff and Vaughn (1980), using the same sample, demonstrated that patients from low EE families who relapse were much more likely to experience an undesirable life event, suggesting that relapse is predicted either by high EE or a stressful life event, suggesting they are functionally equivalent. Leff and Vaughn (1980) found that although maintenance medication was beneficial in preventing relapse in high but not low EE homes over 9 months, this was reversed over 2 years (i.e., medication became protective in low but not in high EE homes).

## The prospective studies

There are now well over 26 prospective studies of the role of EE as a risk factor for relapse in schizophrenia from countries as diverse as Japan, the United Kingdom, Switzerland, and the USA. The research designs are rather similar and draw on the earlier British work. Usually a sample of people with schizophrenia who have experienced acute relapse or a first episode are identified; the CFI is administered and rated to establish families' EE; and patients are followed up for a period of 9 months or a year and monitored for signs of relapse. Relatives are divided into high and low expressed emotion and in some studies only the "key" relative is assigned an EE status, whereas other studies measure all close relatives.

Bebbington and Kuipers (1994) reported a meta-analysis of these studies using data obtained from the original authors, totalling in all 1346 patients. They were able to determine first of all that the proportion of high EE families is approximately 52%, with 62% in high contact with the patient of whom 60% were male. Overall relapse in the high EE families averaged 50%, while in low EE cases it was 21%, which was highly statistically significant.

Bebbington and Kuipers were also able to determine that the effect is apparent whether the patient is receiving medication or not or whether the patient is male or female. Those in high contact with a high EE family show a higher rate of relapse (58% vs 42%) but the size of this effect is much less than the original studies suggested. It was originally thought that those living in a high EE family might not require maintenance medication; however, Bebbington and Kuipers show that EE and medication contribute equally and independently to relapse. These robust findings have inspired a number of intervention studies which have demonstrated a reduction in the rate of relapse (see Chapter 8) and further contribute to the validity of the expressed emotion concept.

## What is EE?

The expressed emotion findings remain essentially empirical: there is no guiding theory and, in fact, theoretical developments have tended to follow these empirical data. It is important to remember that EE is a measure of relatives' interview behaviour and is therefore remote from actual life. However, the ability of a "one-off" measure to predict relapse over 12 months does suggest that there is something *enduring* about it.

The question remains, however, why are some families high in EE?

One approach argues that relatives have difficulty coping with someone whose behaviour has changed considerably, for example, with the negative and positive symptoms. This has been studied by a number of authors and high EE relatives report both a perceived difficulty in coping and their options for coping appear more limited (Birchwood, & Cochrane, 1990). It is possible that this arises because high EE relatives experience greater burden (Birchwood et al., 1992; Scazufca, & Kuipers, 1996), have more behavioural difficulties to cope with (Brown et al., 1972), or that high EE relatives are themselves more isolated from effective social support, though the evidence for the latter is limited (Bebbington, & Kuipers, 1994). Coping difficulty then is a major theme among high EE relatives.

Misattribution is another theme: there is strong evidence that high EE relatives tend to attribute behavioural changes (e.g., withdrawal) to the person ("he's lazy") rather than to the illness ("it's negative symptoms"), thus attracting blame and criticism. This has been studied extensively (Barrowclough, Tarrier, & Johnston, 1996) with consistently positive findings. The idea here is that the person is attributed as having some control over these behaviours, hence the use of criticisms directed towards the person rather than the illness. However, it should be borne in mind that criticism of the individual is intrinsic to the definition of high expressed emotion, and the results are perhaps a tautology.

Birchwood and Smith (1987) have argued that high EE is not a trait of families but a characteristic that develops with time as a result of difficulty in coping with the onset of major illness; in other words, it does not signify a pathology of families but problems in adjustment. They point to the data which suggest that high EE is poorly predictive of relapse in first episode schizophrenic patients (MacMillan, Gold, Crow, Johnson, & Johnstone, 1986: Stirling, Tantam, Newby et al., 1993) and that high EE is not stable over time (Tarrier et al., 1988). They argue that the early phase of psychosis witnesses a period of maximum adjustment and change; they attribute primacy to relatives' beliefs about the illness and to their sense of "loss" of the individual they once knew. As alluded to in Chapter 1, grief reactions have been well documented in psychosis (Miller et al., 1991) and they speculate that some relatives fail to resolve their sense of loss, and that in order to deal with this the patient is attributed with greater responsibility for their inability to return to normal thus easing the emotional distress on the relative. Stirling, Tantam, Newby et al. (1993) observed that criticism evolves over time, often beginning with a high level of emotional over-involvement (EOI). Patterson, Birchwood and Cochrane (2000) suggested that EOI is a manifestation of loss but, when unresolved, it turns to anger and criticism, and thus a high number of critical comments. It is however virtually certain that the pattern of high EE-related behaviour and repeated relapse represents a vicious circle and the "family causes relapse" idea is a gross oversimplification: EE should be viewed as a result of *interactions* between carer and patient (Birchwood, & Smith, 1987; Scazufca, & Kuipers, 1998) over a long period of time.

## The influence of ethnicity and culture

The similarity in the form of schizophrenia in culturally hetero-geneous countries has been noted earlier in this book. It was also discussed in Chapter 2 whether the prognosis for schizophrenia is also comparable across cultures. Common sense suggests that the outcome for schizophrenia will, if at all, be somewhat better in western countries due to the availability of better resources to fund treatment and services. In fact, as noted previously, the research consistently points in the opposite direction (Warner, 1994).

The first well-controlled cross-cultural study was reported by Murphy and Rahman (1971). These authors followed up British and Mauritian first admission samples ($N$ = 90 and 100 respectively) over 5 and 12 years. The groups were matched on important variables, including diagnostic characteristics. They found that the same proportion (30%) of each sample developed a chronic, unremitting disorder; however, whereas 68% of the Mauritian sample showed no further relapse after the first episode, only 32% of the British sample did so. In an attempt to control for ethnicity they studied a similar population inhabiting the westernised Virgin Islands and found that they too showed an inferior course compared with the Mauritians. In 1979, Elaine Waxler followed up a sample of first admission schizophrenic patients in another developing country, Sri Lanka, finding that after 5 years nearly half had no further episodes of schizophrenia, which by western standards is a very high recovery rate. Kulhara and Wig (1978), in a 6-year follow-up of patients in rural India, also found that 41% of their sample had not relapsed; however, this study showed a high rate of attrition of the sample at follow-up (43%).

The most reliable cross-cultural comparisons have come from reports of the International Pilot Study of Schizophrenia (IPSS; WHO, 1973) in which over 1000 patients from nine countries were followed up using standard assessments, diagnostic criteria and follow-up procedures. On all measures the developing countries show *superior* outcome. Once again the difference mainly occurs as a result of the large proportion of patients who do *not* relapse in the developing countries. Indeed, so strong was this (unpredicted) effect that the well-established prognostic distinction between schizophrenic and affective psychoses did not materialise in the developing countries.

The problems of achieving true comparability of sampling, measurement, outcome, and other criteria across cultures has been further addressed in the trans-cultural research programme of WHO. This was the epidemiologically based study of first episodes of psychosis covering 10 countries (Jablensky et al., 1992). This study found a uniform annual incidence rate for schizophrenia (10 per 100,000) but a variable 2-year outcome between countries, once again favouring less industrialised nations. On five of the six outcome variables, patients in developing countries "had a markedly better prognosis" than patients in the developed countries.

For example, 49% of patients in Chandigarh, India, showed a complete remission after their first psychotic episode compared with only 29% of patients in Nottingham, England (Jablensky et al., 1992). These results are a reverse of what might have been anticipated given the greater use of neuroleptic medication and better resourced service infrastructure in the developed countries. Known prognostic variables including mode of onset, gender, illicit drug use, and clinical characteristics could not account for the overall effect. As Edgerton and Cohen (1994) have indicated, the strength of these large data sets needs to be set against the absence of any direct measures of culture. Developing countries are culturally heterogeneous; and it cannot be assumed that activities such as work or more prosaic variables such as family size can easily be compared across cultures (Karno and Jenkins, 1993). Quantitative and qualitative analyses need to go hand in hand and indeed the WHO (1979) report concludes that "epidemiological and cross cultural investigations using an interdisciplinary approach to the study of smaller subgroups are likely to form the most productive strategy in the future."

In view of the wide number of countries contributing to this effect it seems reasonable to suppose that the answer lies within the culture itself and its response to schizophrenia, rather than an intrinsic characteristic of the patients themselves. Some study of the societal structure of these developing countries and their response to mental disorder has been undertaken by social anthropologists (Murphy, 1978; Waxler, 1979), and may be summarised as follows:

1. Societal structure is predominantly rural and agrarian and the functional economic unit tends to be the village rather than the

family and indeed the boundary between family and village life is often blurred. Thus roles are assigned within the village to maintain its functional integrity, independence, and economic viability.

2. Families are able to reintegrate the individual back into community life through the provision of a useful social role and are assisted in this because their relatives have greater influence over the means of economic production. In contrast, socio-economic features of western countries, such as the view of labour as a marketable commodity, the prevalence of unemployment and the technical sophistication required of workers, places schizophrenic patients with residual symptoms at a particular disadvantage.

3. Abnormal behaviour is tolerated to a greater degree, although families are aware that they are tolerating disturbance (i.e., families' reports of "abnormal" behaviour concord with professional evaluations). Such tolerance does not prevent them seeking treatment however (see Waxler, 1979).

4. Families retain greater control over the treatment of the individual and may terminate it if they are dissatisfied. Support for the patient from family and community is strong.

In the light of anthropological observations Murphy (1978) and others have argued that the prevalent view in developing countries of the "curability" or transience of schizophrenia does not lead to the inculcation of an illness or sick role which the patients act out. This view has its origin in labelling theory which holds that labels (e.g., "psychiatric patient") carry with them certain expectations of behaviour which the recipient carries out once he or she has accepted the label. Labelling theory itself has been questioned as a coherent account of schizophrenia (Cochrane, 1983): However, the belief in the transience of the disorder must surely enhance the confidence and self-image of patients, which in turn may have consequences for their psychological adjustment.

The different experiences of patients following discharge from hospital, particularly the superior support and social reintegration apparently available in developing countries, suggests that a more accepting environment with the availability of a useful but perhaps undemanding occupational role is much less likely to place excessive stress on patients. And stress is a factor that appears to influence relapse. Indeed, the environmental factors which have been observed to influence outcome *within* cultures, i.e., life stress, family reactions, community or social reintegration, and social support, all seem to be more favourable in the developing countries and, collectively, could contribute to the superior outcome for schizophrenia.

The opportunity for such a study exists in the UK where there is a large population of Asian immigrants who strongly retain their cultural identities and maintain close extended family networks. A comparison of the prognosis for schizophrenia between white and immigrant cultural groups, and its link with psychosocial factors, would be instructive. A number of such investigations have been reported in the UK. For example, a study based on hospital admission statistics by Cochrane and Singh Bal (1987) found that Pakistani and Indian-born patients living in the UK had a lower rate of readmission to hospital than the white population. In another study of 125 first episode Asian, White, and Afro Caribbean British patients in Birmingham (Birchwood et al., 1992), it was found that the rate of relapse over 12 months was much lower among the Asian (16%) compared with White (30%) and Afro Caribbean (49%) patients. The total amount of time spent as an inpatient was much shorter among the Asian group as a result of this lower rate of readmission. This study also found that nearly 90% of the Asian patients remained with their close family (including half who were married) compared with 70% for Whites and 31% for Afro Caribbeans. When these differences in family structure were controlled, group differences in outcome were no longer significant.

These data support the notion that part of the effect of ethnicity may be accounted for by stability of family and kinship ties. These studies bring us back to the research on expressed emotion (EE): do families living in developing countries show lower levels of EE, are they therefore less critical, hostile, and involved with respect to the person with schizophrenia. The expressed emotion among extended families of patients in Chandigarh was studied by Leff, Wig, Ghosh et al. (1990), who found a much lower prevalence of high EE families (23%) compared with London (47%). Similarly, the extended family structure of Mexican-American families has been shown to be associated with lower prevalence of high EE compared with families living in the UK and US (Karno, Jenkins, de la Selva et al., 1987).

There is strong evidence that there are powerful and robust differences in the outcome for schizophrenia favouring less industrialised countries and that this effect may be partly explained by a stable and intact extended family structure that can offer support and containment. The availability of a valued productive social role (of which paid employment is but one example) has been regarded as a crucial prognostic factor relevant to these cross-cultural differences (Kleinman, 1987), and has been observed within cultures (MacMillan et al., 1986). There is evidence from the WHO studies that social reintegration, particularly the availability of socially valued and productive roles, is more common in India. The WHO field workers in India for example reported some difficulties in interviewing patients at follow-up as many were busy at work (men) or in domestic activity (women). If there is greater opportunity for role-appropriate behaviour, either through reintegration into a domestic pattern based upon extended kinship reciprocal obligation and or via the patient being re-involved in a family-run enterprise without the need to compete for formal employment, then this may also contribute to the observed differences in outcome (see also Chapter 7).

It has been over 30 years since Wing and Bennett's initial observation that the social environment, if overstimulating, might raise the risk of psychotic relapse. After more than three decades of research we can have confidence that, by and large, this is indeed a robust conclusion. Stressful life events, intensive and perhaps hostile relationships occurring within families, and, more broadly, the wider societal response including that of tolerance and support appear to be key influences affecting the course of psychotic illness and the quality of life of those affected.

## Summary

- There is an interaction between intrinsic vulnerability to psychosis and stress. This is called the "stress–vulnerability model".
- Life events and stress arising from family life raise the risk of relapse.
- There is no evidence that difficult family relationships alone are a cause of schizophrenia; however, they may be a risk factor.
- The outcome for schizophrenia in developing countries is better than in the developed, industralised nations.

# Psychological aspects 5

In this chapter, three different psychological approaches to understanding schizophrenia are described: positive symptoms theories, neuropsychological theories, and theories of psychosis proneness.

There have been a number of attempts to find a unified psychological theory to explain the complex array of symptoms and phenomena that defines schizophrenia (Arieti, 1955; Bateson, Jackson, Haley, & Weakland, 1956; Fromm-Reichman, 1948). By and large these have been unsuccessful; recently there has been a move away from all-encompassing psychological models and theories to those attempting to explain and understand the specific components or symptoms of schizophrenia and psychosis (Bentall, 1990; Costello, 1992). It is these theories that are the subject of this chapter.

## Psychological theories of positive symptoms

Delusions and hallucinations are perhaps the best known of all the symptoms of schizophrenia. Despite this and a century of study, these "positive" symptoms (see Chapter 1) remain poorly understood. It is important to understand that the positive symptoms of schizophrenia are played out in the mental arena where they are subjected to the vast array of processes common to all mental acts. It is therefore difficult to understand why *psychological* theories have been so slow to influence our understanding and treatment of delusions and hallucinations. This is now beginning to change, a situation that has encouraged the development of a number of psychological interventions that directly address the alleviation of distress associated with psychotic symptoms.

## Psychological theories and models of delusions

Delusions have until recently been subject to relatively little psychological research. This is surprising bearing in mind the wealth of studies looking at the formation and maintenance of ordinary beliefs and belief structures (Tesser, & Shaffer, 1990) and the central role that delusions play in diagnostic systems and more general definitions of madness (Winters, & Neale, 1983). For example, delusions have always been present in the legal definition of mental illness (Sims, 1991).

Defining what a delusion is, however, is notoriously difficult. One traditional approach has been to establish qualitative differences between delusions and other beliefs. Thus, for instance, in *DSM-III-R*, forerunner to *DSM IV*, (*The Diagnostic and Statistical Manual* of the American Psychiatric Association), which originally appeared in 1987, a delusion is defined as:

> a false personal belief based on incorrect inference about external reality and firmly sustained in spite of what everyone else believes and in spite of what constitutes incontrovertible and obvious proof or evidence to the contrary. The belief is not one ordinarily accepted by other members of the person's culture.

Although this appears intuitively correct, closer analysis casts some doubt on true qualitative differences between delusions and other strongly held beliefs, e.g., that God exists. There appears to be a case for suggesting that delusions may share more similarity than differences with "normal" beliefs. Thus, traditional criteria have been challenged by radical attempts to define delusions as points on a continuum with normality, the position on this continuum being influenced by the degree of conviction in the belief, and the extent of preoccupation with the belief (Strauss, 1969). It is for such reasons that the last 20 years or so have seen a shift in emphasis away from discontinuity to continuity and from qualitative to quantitative difference between normal and abnormal beliefs. Paranoid thinking, for example, can be detected in ordinary people (Rawlings, & Freeman, 1996) and may even be socially adaptive!

It is possible to divide cognitive and psychological theories of delusions into two camps: those advocating that they are underpinned by abnormal cognitive deficits (i.e., in reasoning, attention, or memory) and those arguing that they are the product of abnormal *perceptions*. Typical of the former view is Bentall's model of paranoid delusions. Bentall and his colleagues, like Ziegler and Glick (1988) before them, argue, much like the psychoanalysts, that paranoid and persecutory delusions act as a psychological defence against depression and low self-esteem, and that such a defence process is maintained by attention and memory biases. These issues may include selective attention to threat-related stimuli (Bentall, & Kaney, 1989; Kinderman, 1994), biased recall of threat-related cues (Kaney, Wolfenden, Dewey, & Bentall, 1992), and bias in attributional style, which blames negative outcomes on external causes (Bentall, Kaney, & Dewey, 1991). Thus, Bentall and colleagues propose that persecutory delusions may arise as a consequence of abnormal cognitive biases that are triggered by the motivation to explain perceived discrepancies between actual (who they believe they are) and ideal (who they would like to be) self following a negative event (i.e., failing to get a job), in order to maintain self-esteem. For example, according to Bentall, Kaney, Kinderman, and colleagues, a person with persecutory delusions is likely to construct those delusions ("people are out to get me") unconsciously in order to protect them from thinking negatively about themselves and therefore becoming depressed. These researchers have attempted to support their model by two sets of experimental evidence relating to (1) attributional style and (2) discrepancies between conscious (overt) and unconscious (covert) self-esteem.

In the former, Bentall and colleagues have hypothesised that an attributional style characterised by blaming other people for bad events and taking credit for good events should be evident in people with persecutory delusions but not in other clinical groups (e.g., depressed people) or nonpatient samples. In a number of experiments they have attempted to measure differences in attributions by means of different attribution style questionnaires (Bentall et al., 1991; Kinderman, & Bentall, 1996; Peterson et al., 1982). A typical example of a question that would appear on one of these questionnaires would be "You get a pay rise, write down one major cause for the event". This could then be rated amongst other dimensions on whether it was internal (i.e., "due to my hard work") or external ("the company had a good year"). Internality is a measure of how much the person thinks that good and bad events are due to something about him or her; externality on the other hand is an indication of how much the person believes it is due to other people or circumstances.

Overall, evidence from these experiments does suggest that when compared with depressed and nonclinical control groups, people with persecutory delusions display a bias to external personal attributions for negative events (Sharp, Fear, & Healy, 1997). There is not, however, strong evidence that they attribute good events (i.e., getting a job) to internal factors about themselves or bad events to situational or chance factors. Thus, when faced with certain situations that might reflect upon them, people with persecutory delusions are more likely to see others as responsible for bad events (Garety, & Freeman, 1999). The second piece of empirical evidence testing the paranoid hypomesis comes from studies examining the discrepancies between reported self-esteem and covertly measured self-esteem. Drawing upon the work of Higgins (1987), Bentall and colleagues have argued that people are motivated to preserve a positive view of themselves by reducing as much as possible, the gap between how they perceive themselves (actual self) and how they would like to be seen (ideal self). It is proposed that where this gap is large there will be a tendency to view themselves negatively. In contrast, positive views of themselves (high self-esteem) are associated with a close association between actual and ideal self. With this in mind, it is argued by Bentall and colleagues that the tendency towards external attributional bias in people with persecutory delusions minimises the awareness of the gulf between actual and ideal self and thereby maintains self-esteem. In essence, it is predicted that people with persecutory delusions will, if asked directly, deny there is any discrepancy between who they are and who they want to be (actual–ideal self); however, if self-esteem is assessed in a covert way to break the psychological defence, then a large discrepancy between actual and ideal self will be found. Unfortunately, the evidence to date does not appear to support this hypothesis for *all* people with persecutory delusions. It may, however, apply to a subgroup (Garety, & Freeman, 1999) and points to the important role that self-esteem might play in the formation and maintenance of delusions in some people. Improving the self-esteem of people with delusions is an important first step in psychological interventions, before tackling directly their delusional beliefs (Trower, & Chadwick, 1995). Garety, Hemsley, and colleagues have proposed that delusions, in part, may be the product of specific reasoning biases. For example, Huq, Garety, and Hemsley (1988) showed that delusional patients when compared with psychiatric and nonpsychiatric controls have a tendency to "jump to conclusions" when faced with particular problem-solving tasks. In summarising the evidence from 14 experimental studies testing whether people with delusions do demonstrate reasoning biases, Garety and Freeman (1999) conclude that: "a picture emerges of people with delusions showing a tendency to seek less information to reach a decision, but not, when presented with information, being unable to use it" (p. 131).

Thus, according to these authors, people with delusions have a "data-gathering bias" because they are more willing to accept a hypothesis on the basis of less evidence than clinical and nonclinical control groups. This ties in with the common clinical observation that people with delusions often "jump to conclusions" on the basis of specific environmental events (e.g., cars parked on either side of the street with two men in them) or internal experience (e.g., "voices" saying "we're going to get you"). Addressing such reasoning biases in psychological therapy, therefore, would be important.

Psychological theories of delusions which place emphasis upon *abnormal perceptions*, or *experiences*, argue that delusions are normal and rational explanations of abnormal internal events (e.g., hallucinations). Probably the best example of this approach is Maher's "anomalous" experience model (1974). Maher's theory has five main points. (1) The cognitive processes responsible for the formation of *normal* beliefs are the same as those identified in delusional belief formation. (2) Delusions, like all beliefs, serve the purpose of providing order and meaning to the world (i.e., they serve as a type of "mini-theory" for the person). (3) Such mini-theories are needed when events are not predictable. (4) Even delusional explanations for unpredictable, discrepant events bring relief even if the delusional explanation does not fit all the data. Information that conflicts with this view will be either ignored or reinterpreted. (5) The belief will be judged delusional by others if it is based on observations of the environment or internal personal experience that are unavailable to direct observation by others (e.g., "someone has placed a curse on me"). As evidence for his theory, Maher cites studies demonstrating the presence of delusions in a wide range of disorders in which the deluded individuals have no prior history of cognitive impairment (Manschreck, 1979). There is also evidence that delusions can be induced in normal subjects undergoing anomalous experiences (Zimbardo, Anderson, & Kabat, 1981). Finally (and we will return to this in Chapter 8) Maher's model has provided a framework for psychological therapy for delusions, which in some cases has had positive results (Chadwick, & Lowe, 1990).

In summary, the psychological theories of delusions are, on their own, inadequate to explain the complexities surrounding the onset and maintenance of delusions in schizophrenia. However, attributional and reasoning biases do appear to play an important role in explaining why delusions are maintained.

## Psychological theories of auditory hallucinations

Auditory hallucinations are extremely common in people diagnosed with schizophrenia. In the World Health Organisation's International Pilot Study of Schizophrenia (IPSS; WHO, 1973) auditory hallucinations were reported by 73% of people diagnosed as having an acute episode of schizophrenia. They can also be reported by individuals who have seen sexually abused, or suffered a bereavement, as well as individuals diagnosed as having a manic depressive illness or an affective psychosis. Indeed, because they feature in many different disorders, the diagnostic importance of auditory hallucinations has been doubted (Asaad, & Shapiro, 1986).

In addition, it appears that auditory hallucinations are not restricted to clinical groups. Auditory hallucinations have been reported by individuals who, while showing signs of a specific clinical disorder, display insufficient symptoms for a firm diagnosis to be made (Cochrane, 1983). Again, it appears that under laboratory conditions many ordinary people display a propensity to report hearing sounds that are not there, prompting researchers to speculate that the proneness to hallucinate may be a predisposition spread across the general population (Slade, & Bentall, 1988; see also the section on psychosis proneness later in this chapter). Current opinion in psychology veers towards accepting the possibility that hallucinations lie on the continuum with normality (Strauss, 1969).

All psychological theories of hallucinations have one thing in common; they assume that hallucinations occur when people mistake their own internal, mental, or private events for external, publicly observable events (Bentall, 1990). That is, the imaginary is mistaken for the reality. Any psychological theory, therefore, should throw light upon the mechanisms that allow people to differentiate between imagined events and events in the real word. A breakdown of such reality discrimination would, it is assumed, cause a person to misattribute internal events to an external source and thereby bring about an hallucination (Bentall, & Slade, 1985; Morrison, & Haddock, 1997). For instance, Baker and Morrison (1998) compared the attributional biases of 15 people with a diagnosis of schizophrenia who were experiencing auditory hallucinations, with both non-hallucinating schizophrenics and a nonpsychotic control group. Results indicated that patients experiencing hallucinations had a significantly greater tendency to misattribute internal events to an external source as measured by response to a word association task, than those in the two control groups.

## Slade and Bentall's five-factor theory of hallucinations

Slade and Bentall have postulated that hallucinators have a propensity to engage in what they call "sensory deception" whereby they fail to discriminate between self-generated and external sources of information. In addition they argue that people who hallucinate are more likely to be tolerant of ambiguous stimuli and have a tendency to "jump to perception"; to assume quickly that it has an external source (Garety, 1991; Slade, & Bentall, 1988). Their five-factor model specifies that the following factors lead to the onset of hallucinations:

1. Stress-induced arousal.
2. Predisposing factors (e.g., cognitive deficiencies such as suggestibility; Young, Bentall, Slade, & Dewey, 1987).
3. Environmental stimulation.
4. Reinforcement.
5. Expectancy.

It is proposed by Slade and Bentall that heightened arousal induced by stress may promote hallucinatory activity by interfering with the person's ability to process information effectively and thereby increasing the difficulty of discriminating illusion from reality.

Slade and Bentall (1988) argue that some individuals are more predisposed to experiencing hallucinations than others and there is a growing body of evidence suggesting that hallcinators are more likely to respond to suggestions to hear voices than nonhallucinating control subjects (Young et al., 1987); they are more "suggestable". This model also agrees that there is a relationship between *environmental stimulation* and the onset of hallucinations. Both sensory deprivation (e.g., an extremely quiet room) or unpatterned stimulation (e.g., traffic noise), it is argued, are the most likely conditions under which hallucinations will occur. This would help explain why sensory loss in some older people may make them particularly vulnerable to hallucinations (Hammeke, McQuillen, & Cohen, 1983) and why, on the other hand, encouraging hallucinators to concentrate on a meaningful stimulus can be used as an effective coping strategy to help reduce the intensity of voices (Margo, Hemsley, & Slade, 1981).

Although not completely understood it is suggested that hallucinating may be strengthened through *reinforcement*. Slade and Bentall (1988) cite evidence to suggest that hallucinations may bring relief to the person by reducing their anxiety (Slade, 1973). This, however, is inconsistent with more recent findings that show an increase in anxious arousal following hallucinations (Chadwick, & Birchwood, 1994; Close, & Garety, 1998). Although attempts were made to accommodate these contradictory findings, Slade and Bentall admit that it is still not fully understood how, if at all, hallucinators are benefited by their misperceptions. Finally, it has been suggested that people are more likely to see or hear what they are told exists. Thus, in certain cultures hallucinatory phenomena may be approved or actually sought out (Al-Issa, 1995). For instance, in San Juan, Puerto Rico, individuals experiencing hallucinations are more likely to be thought of as being visited by spirits who manifest themselves visually and audibly, and not necessarily as suffering from a mental illness (Warner, 1994).

## Chadwick and Birchwood's model of hallucinations

A different approach, and one aimed at understanding and alleviating the distress caused by "voices" (as opposed to understanding how voices start) has been proposed by Chadwick and Birchwood (1994; Birchwood, & Chadwick, 1997).

The experience of hearing voices is a powerful one that demands a reaction. However, the experience is also very personal. Although it is known that a common first reaction to voices is puzzlement (Maher, 1988), individuals evolve different ways of interacting with their voices. Certain people, for example, experience voices as immensely distressing and frightening and will shout and swear at them; in contrast, others find their voices reassuring and amusing and actually seek contact. Again, in the case of imperative voices, many individuals desperately resist their commands, and comply only at times of great pressure, whereas others comply willingly and fully.

This diversity in the way individuals relate to their voices illustrates the point that voices are not necessarily a problem to the individual concerned; indeed, it is fairly common for individuals to believe their voices to be a solution to a problem. This in turn draws attention to the point that the serious disturbance associated with voices, as with so many other symptoms, tends to be located in the way an individual feels and behaves towards them. People who hear voices often seek or accept help because they are desperate, depressed, angry, or suicidal.

Traditional treatment approaches involve eliminating the experience of voices; Chadwick and Birchwood argue that what causes distress is what patients *believe* about them. Chadwick and Birchwood

(1994; Birchwood, & Chadwick, 1997) propose a cognitive model that places emphasis not upon the content of an auditory hallucination (what a "voice" says), but on what beliefs the patient holds about the voice, e.g., "I can't stop this voice", "If I don't do as it tells me something bad will happen". This includes its identity and purpose— "the devil is punishing me". They argue that people's beliefs about their voices can be summarised under the headings power, identity, and meaning (Chadwick, Birchwood, & Trower, 1996). Beliefs in the power of a voice usually refer to the appraisals the individual makes about how much they can control the voice (i.e., "can I start or stop it?") and how much they believe they need to comply with the voice ("If I ignore this voice it will go on and on and never shut up?"). The voice hearer will usually cite evidence to back up these beliefs ("When I tried ignoring the voice last week it threatened to harm me"). A belief in the power of a voice may be strengthened further by the impression that is often given by auditory hallucinations that they know all about a person's past, their perceived weaknesses, and their current thoughts, feelings, and behaviours. For instance, one voice hearer describes how he believed his voice to be powerful because it knew about an incident that occurred when he was 14, when he had been caught stealing from a shop.

Beliefs in the *identity and meaning* of an auditory hallucination, it is argued, will also influence how the person reacts to the voice. For instance, if a person believes his voice emanated from the devil he will react to it differently than if he thinks it comes from his friend. Often the content of the voice (i.e., what the voice says) is used as evidence by the person for the source of the voice. Many voices identify themselves or provide clues to the identity as a powerful being (i.e., making threats or putting people down). Birchwood and Chadwick (1997) provide strong support for the cognitive model.

# Neuropsychological models of schizophrenia

Unlike psychological theories aimed at explaining the maintenance of specific psychotic symptoms such as delusions and hallucinations, neuropsychological models of schizophrenia seek to explain underlying vulnerabilities and how biological impairments may give rise to psychotic experiences. That is, neuropsychological theories are concerned with the way the brain works and, in psychosis, how it can go wrong. Some neuropsychological theories of schizophrenia are based on the idea that the symptoms of the disorder are the products of a defect in selective attention (McKenna, 1997), a fault in the filtering system, which allows us to choose what we will attend to (internal and external) and allow into our conscious awareness. Many researchers over the years have proposed that people with schizophrenia report changes in the nature of their conscious experience including heightened perception and awareness of the environment, increased subjective alertness, the ability of seemingly irrelevant material to capture their attention, and over-inclusive thinking.

Impairment in attention and concentration can make it difficult for people with schizophrenia to concentrate in conversation and process what they are saying. (Davidson et al., 1998). McGhie and Chapman (1961, pp. 105–106) illustrated this point with an account of a person with schizophrenia describing some of his difficulties.

> If there are three or four people talking at one time I can't take it in. I would not be able to hear what they are saying [properly] and I would get the one mixed up with the other.
>
> To me it's just like a bubble—a noise that goes right through me.

Two of the best-known neuropsychological theories of schizophrenia today are those proposed by Frith and Hemsley. Frith's model (1992) is an attempt to explain the onset and maintenance of positive symptoms. Frith (1987; see Chapter 1) has proposed that people with schizophrenia display cognitive deficits that do not allow them to distinguish between actions that derive from external stimuli and those that are driven by internal intentions. That is, there is a breakdown (due to a number of causes) in the brain process that provides a cognitive method allowing one to distinguish automatically between internally and externally generated events. Frith hypothesises that such deficits may be the result of an irregularity in the neuronal pathways connecting the septo-hippocampal system with the prefrontal cortex. Problems in the regulation of the neurotransmitter dopamine in this part of the brain would, it is predicted, give rise to psychotic symptoms under certain circumstances (see, for instance, stress–vulnerability models in Chapter 4). It is a particularly powerful explanation of passivity experiences (feelings or experience of being controlled by external forces) and third-person auditory hallucinations (hearing voices speaking about you or commenting on your actions). Frith further argues that thinking is normally accompanied by a sense of "effort" and deliberate choice as we switch from one thought to the next. In schizophrenia, Frith suggests such the sense of "effort" is diminished. This would go some way to explaining why some of the positive symptoms of psychosis such as thought insertion (which have not been subjected to "central monitoring") appear to originate from external alien forces (Frith, 1992).

Frith (1992) has suggested that schizophrenia may share one of the common cognitive defects found in autism: an inability to achieve an understanding that other people have a mental state, or "theory of mind".

> the autistic person has never known that other people have minds. The schizophrenic knows well that other people have minds, but has lost the ability to infer the contents of these minds: their beliefs and intentions. They may even lose the ability to reflect on the contents of their own mind.
>
> (Frith, 1992, p. 121)

Not only does Frith note some of the similarities between the negative symptoms of schizophrenia and autism (social withdrawal, impoverished communication), he also argues that such a deficiency in theory of mind may help to explain why delusions are formed. An inability to understand the intentions of other people could lead a person to make incorrect inferences, becoming puzzled and thereby suspicious of the intentions of others.

Undoubtedly Frith's model has provided us with a comprehensive neuropsychological framework for many of the symptoms observed in schizophrenia, with what appears to be considerable explanatory power. Unfortunately, empirical evidence for the theory is still not great (Penn, Corrigan, Bentall, Racestein, & Newman, 1997). Some (Fowler, Garety, & Kuipers, 1995) have criticised it on the grounds that it is too reductionistic and does not take into account the role of environmental influences.

## Hemsley's model

Another attempt at a comprehensive account of the vulnerabilities underlying symptoms of schizophrenia from a neuropsychological perspective has been provided by Hemsley (1993a). In contrast to Frith, Hemsley argues that the abnormalities of behaviour and experience characteristic of schizophrenia correspond to a breakdown in the normal relationship between memory and current sensory input. In other words, perception and memory become interwoven. As a result, it is suggested that people with schizophrenia are impaired in their ability to choose between relevant and irrelevant sensory information from their environment. As this will usually occur quickly and automatically, the person is likely to remain unaware that they may be attending to seemingly superfluous aspects of the social environment but interpreting them as highly significant (e.g., a car horn is seen as being personally relevant to them and containing a message). Conversely, Hemsley also suggests that such a cognitive deficit would lead to thoughts being accessed automatically from memory, which are then perceived as irrelevant and alien to the person's goals and expectancies. It is then more likely that this "alien" sensation will be attributed to an external source such as a voice (i.e., auditory hallucinations).

Hemsley has attempted to marry his cognitive model with an underlying neurological system (Gray, Feldon, Rawlins, Hemsley, & Smith, 1990). This proposes that abnormalities of the hippocampus and related brain structures may be central to the emergence of psychotic symptoms. It has been argued that the hippocampus plays a vital role in the comparison of actual and expected stimuli (Gray, 1982). The hippocampus, according to Gray, is responsible for the moment by moment generation of predictions of subsequent sensory input, something that Hemsley has proposed has broken down in schizophrenia and may account for the abnormal perception and abnormal reasoning that characterise the illness. Again, unequivocal evidence for Hemsley's model is still outstanding but limited laboratory studies and animal experiments have been consistent with the theory (Hemsley, 1994). Like Frith's model, however, it clearly points to the idea that abnormalities of information processing within schizophrenia are most likely to lead to daily problems in everyday cognitive tasks which many people take for granted: problems with learning and remembering things, difficulties with interpersonal interactions and relationships (Davidson et al., 1998). Unfortunately, such cognitive and social disabilities are often poorly understood by relatives, friends, and the patients themselves. This is especially true when they are masked by intact verbal skills and other talents (Fowler et al., 1995). When working with people with schizophrenia, it is important to deflect a sense of blame from the person with schizophrenia and to make all concerned aware of any possible changes in cognitive and social functioning.

# Psychological proneness—schizotypy and schizotypal personality disorder

It has been suggested that the changes in the social and cognitive functioning that are so often witnessed in schizophrenia may be apparent prior to the emergence of the illness (Claridge, 1997). Over the years there have been many different approaches to the study of "psychosis proneness" or "schizotypy" (Meehl, 1962). Claridge (1997) suggests that the features of psychotic disorders such as schizophrenia lie on a continuum with normal behaviour and experience. Although he argues that "schizotypal traits" associated with psychotic disorders may predispose an individual to schizophrenia on the one hand, they may also lead to positive outcomes such as enhanced creativity and spiritual experience.

Drawing upon comparisons with systemic disorders in physical medicine such as the hypertension-related diseases, Claridge (1990, p. 163) argues that there is an "inescapable connection between illness and health".

Schizotypy, like blood pressure, would be expected to show individual variation within the normal population. Under certain circumstances, however, certain triggering factors may increase the risk of illness. For blood pressure, triggers may be such things as stress, diet, smoking, and alcohol, eventually leading to raised blood pressure, hypertension, and increased risk of stroke and heart failure. (See also Chapter 4: Stress-vulnerability models.)

The psychosis-proneness approach offers perhaps the best explanation for why there may be a spectrum of schizophrenia-related disorders such as schizotypal personality disorder and other borderline states. Schizotypal personality disorder shares many of the characteristics of schizophrenia but in a milder form (i.e., difficulties in interpersonal relationships as well as abnormalities of thought, behaviour, and appearance; Raine, Lencz, & Mednick, 1995). Although in the United Kingdom there has been more emphasis on the dimensional *personality-based* aspects of schizotypy, in North America, schizotypy is seen as a more disease-based concept—for example, mediated by a single major gene. Although the two views are not completely incompatible, researchers in North America are less convinced by the argument that individuals could ever live satisfactorily with their "psychotic personalities" or see some of the features of schizotypy (i.e., outer body experiences, dream-like states, etc.) in a positive light (Claridge, 1997).

A significant body of evidence from normal adult populations does support the continuum model of schizophrenia, drawing both on questionnaire-based studies (e.g., Bentall, Claridge, & Slade, 1989; Chapman, & Chapman, 1985) and laboratory investigations (Beech et al., 1989). In a typical example Chapman and Chapman (1985) conducted a longitudinal study of hypothetically psychosis-prone individuals (assessed on interview-based and self-report questionnaires designed to measure enduring schizotypal and psychosis-prone traits) to establish whether they would have a heightened incidence of psychosis at a 10-year follow-up evaluation. Those scoring high on psychosis-proneness scales were more likely 10 years later to meet the diagnostic criteria for psychosis; to have more relatives with psychosis and report more psychotic-like experiences than those with low scores. Overall, although the numbers of psychosis-prone people going on to develop the clinical disorder was low (14 out of 182), this and similar studies like it have encouraged a scientific debate that questions the commonly assumed idea that psychosis (especially schizophrenia) is simply "present" or "absent". Some researchers, such as Claridge, turn this idea on its head and suggest that, like intelligence, "psychotic" traits form part of normal individuality. In so doing, this has modified the views of many who previously believed that schizophrenia had a single cause. Instead, there appear to be multiple symptom dimensions along which people, who may be subject to a later psychotic breakdown, will vary.

## Summary

- A number of psychological theories have been proposed to explain some of the psychological processes that may underpin the symptoms of schizophrenia.
- Psychological attempts to explain delusions have advocated both the role of cognitive deficits (i.e., biases in reasoning, attention, and/or memory) and of abnormal perception.
- Psychological theories of hallucinations assume that hallucinations occur when people mistake their own internal events for external observable events.
- Neuropsychological theories for schizophrenia seek to explain how biological impairments may give rise to the cognitive "hardware" deficits that produce the symptoms of schizophrenia.

- Many of the neuropsychological theories have emphasised a defect in the filtering system controlling the processing of information.
- Theories of psychosis proneness (schizotypy) provide evidence to suggest that there may be psychological markers for psychosis that are present prior to the development of the disorder.

# Drug treatment 6

In this chapter we will discuss the use of medication in the management of schizophrenia.

Drug treatment for schizophrenia is now widespread in clinical practice. The era of antipsychotic drugs (referred to as "neuroleptics") began with the discovery of a group of drugs known as the phenothiazines. Phenothiazine was first synthesised in 1883 and made its medical debut in 1934 as a urinary antiseptic and insecticide. A chemical derivative, promethazine, was discovered to possess antihistamine and sedative properties but attempts to sedate agitated patients with it were unsuccessful. Charpentier in Paris synthesised a further derivative, chlorpromazine, which the French surgeon Laborit used in combination with other drugs to improve the action of analgesics. Laborit discovered that chlorpromazine (Largactil) seemed to tranquillise without sedating his surgical patients. In 1952 Delay and Deniker in Paris discovered that chlorpromazine had a therapeutic influence on disturbed agitated patients, alleviating hallucinations and delusions.

This compound and its variants—notably trifluoperazine and fluphenazine—were widely adopted in clinical practice. A chemically similar group of drugs, the thioxanthenes, were later synthesised in Copenhagen by Peterson (e.g., Flupenthixol) and a further, chemically distinct group, butyrophenones, were developed in Belgium by a pharmaceutical company, although now only one of these is widely used and marketed (Haloperidol). These drugs have a number of clinical functions including the treatment of acute episodes of psychosis as a means of preventing relapse, and recently a new group of drugs have become available for individuals whose symptoms are resistant to treatment with the conventional neuroleptics.

# Acute treatment

The control of acute symptoms with neuroleptics is relatively uncontroversial and boasts high clinical efficacy (Freeman, 1978). A large number of randomised, double-blind placebo trials of neuroleptic medication for acute psychosis have been undertaken. These earlier studies were reviewed by Davis and Garver (1978) and, in nine out of ten studies, there was a significant advantage of the active over the placebo neuroleptic. The neuroleptics have been shown to have a very specific impact on the positive symptoms: the hallucinations, delusions, and thought disorders. Considerable heterogeneity in patients' responses to these drugs has also been well documented. Studies of psychosis before the era of the neuroleptics show that there were many individuals who recovered naturally from episodes of psychosis (Bleuler, 1978). There is also a group of patients who fail to recover even though treated with neuroleptic drugs: MacMillan et al. (1986) showed that 6.5% were unable to be discharged after the first hospitalisation owing to the persistence of severe positive symptoms and, in a study of protocol-based acute treatment of the first episode, Loebel, Lieberman, Alvir et al. (1992) found that 16% failed to recover within 1 year of first treatment.

A number of studies have demonstrated that long delays can occur between the onset of psychotic symptoms and the first treatment, averaging 12 months or more (Birchwood, M., McGorry, P., & Jackson, H. 1997); these delays are associated with a doubling of the risk of early relapse (Crow et al., 1986) and an increased likelihood of delay in response to treatment and to the presence of residual symptoms (Loebel et al., 1992). These data suggest that early treatment can improve the initial response to neuroleptics.

The dose of drugs used in acute psychosis has been widely acknowledged to have increased since their introduction; the assumption has been that the higher the dose the better the clinical response even though this risks serious drug side-effects. It has been argued that once patients have reached the "neuroleptic threshold" and begin to experience drug side-effects, this precisely corresponds with the optimum therapeutic dose. In an elegant test of this hypothesis study by McEvoy, Hogarty, and Steingard (1991), patients were provided with a "neuroleptic threshold" dose, which was doubled if the symptoms did not improve within 3 weeks. The results showed that doubling the dose of the neuroleptic (Haloperidol) did not lead to an improved response to treatment. The point here is that even with low doses of neuroleptics—sufficient to give rise to side-effects—an adequate therapeutic response is obtained.

## Side-effects

The side-effects of neuroleptic medication are frequently distressing and prominent among these include acute dystonic reactions (e.g., muscular spasms involving the head and neck affecting vision); akathisia (including restlessness, agitation, fidgeting, rocking, and pacing); Parkinsonism (including stiffness, tremor, shuffling gait, and dribbling); and tardive dyskinesia, which is a side-effect emerging many months after the start of treatment that may consist of involuntary movements of the head and tongue, and can affect speech, posture, and sometimes breathing.

## Relapse prevention

The continued use of neuroleptic medication following acute treatment was advocated because of the high rate of relapse, which in one study was reported to be as high as 80% within 2 years (Hogarty, Goldberg, & Schooler, 1974). The prevention of relapse is indeed critical as not only is it distressing itself, but it can also lead to irreversible social consequences and increases the likelihood of symptoms persisting between major episodes (Shepherd et al., 1989). A landmark study by Leff and Wing (1971) prescribed a low daily dose of an oral neuroleptic in a double-blind trial, which was shown to lead to a 50% reduction in the risk of relapse within 1 year of the acute episode.

Hogarty and Ulrich (1977) studied a regime where maintenance medication of this level was discontinued and found that the mean time before relapse was substantially reduced from 12 to 4.5 months (in other words withdrawing medication increased the risk of relapse). Hogarty and Ulrich also reported that the longer the patient survives without relapse the lower the risk of relapse becomes; thus, in the first few months the risk of relapse for those receiving placebo was 13% (vs 4% for those receiving active medication); by the end of 2 years the relapse figures was 3% for active and 1.5% for placebo. Hogarty and Ulrich also reported that 65% of patients on active medication would eventually relapse compared with 87% of those receiving placebo, which implies that medication will indefinitely prevent relapse in 22% but only postpone it in 65%. This has now become an accepted wisdom—neuroleptics extend the interval between relapses (i.e., they delay relapse) but they do not prevent it.

These data on the preventative qualities of continued low-dose medication led to the introduction of injectable forms: these are oil-based compounds administered by deep intramuscular injection into the gluteal muscle every 2 weeks or so. They diffuse slowly into the bloodstream and ensure continuity of the neuroleptic reaching the brain and are not subject to metabolism by the liver, unlike oral medication. These so-called "depot" injections have become very popular, particularly in Britain, even though the controlled studies show that there is very little difference between oral and injectable preparations in their preventative properties (Barnes, Milavic, Curson, & Plaff, 1983). The main rationale for their use is that they ensure adherence with these regimes. Adherence continues to be a problem, with up to 50% of patients reported to have adherence in maintenance studies of oral medication (Kane, 1987); thus, the advantage of a depot maintenance strategy is one of convenience for the mental health services, and not compliance per se.

Other strategies have developed to reduce the risk of relapse. One of these involves targeting medication at the onset of "early signs" or prodromal symptoms of relapse, which has been shown to be a successful strategy in the context of a continued maintenance medication (Marder, Wirshing, Van Putten et al., 1994) but not as an alternative to regular maintenance medication (Carpenter, Hanlon, Heinrichs et al., 1990)—see Chapter 8 for a review.

## Dose reduction strategies

The continued problems associated with drug side-effects, including the risk of nonadherence to drug regimes and the raised risk of major long-term complications such as tardive dyskinesia, have led to attempts to develop strategies to reduce exposure to neuroleptics without prejudicing their relapse prevention properties.

The main strategy employed here has been to compare the efficacy of standard with very low dose medication regimes. A large double-blind control trial by Kane, Rifkin, & Woerner (1983) randomly allocated 126 patients to receive low dose or standard dose fluphenazine. This low dose strategy led to a seven-fold increase in the relapse rate in the first year in those receiving low doses (relapse rate 56% vs 7%), although patients receiving the low dose rarely required rehospitalisation and the damage associated with the relapse was minimal. There were, however, also major benefits of low doses in terms of improved social contact and improved well-being. A similar trial by Johnson, Ludlow, & Street (1987) compared a standard dose of 40mg depot every 2 weeks with 20mg, and at the end of the first year the relapse rate in the lower dose group was approximately three times higher. This group were followed up over 3 years, which confirmed that the reduction in neuroleptic dose increased significantly the rate of relapse although, by careful monitoring, the relapse could be detected and managed.

There have been a number of attempts to substitute maintenance regimes for targeted or intermittent ones that involve close monitoring of individuals' well-being and reinstitution of medication at the earliest signs of a relapse. The main problem associated with these regimes (Birchwood, 1995) is that this leads to high frequency of unpleasant prodromal symptoms (e.g., low mood, agitation, social withdrawal). Four randomised trials comparing intermittent with standard continuous medication have been reported, including one German multicentre trial (Gaebel, 1995), and the outcome over 2 years reveals a major advantage for continuous treatment over the intermittent regime.

An alternative strategy involves the combined use of low dose maintenance treatment with increased dose at the early signs of relapse. This strategy was used by Marder, Van Putten, Mintz et al. (1987) and, in this as in the follow-up study (Marder et al., 1994), the rate of relapse in the two groups was not significantly different, particularly in the second year of the trial, but the comparison groups were not associated with a significant difference in drug side-effects.

These data suggest that drug withdrawal or low dose regimes are associated with an increased risk of relapse, but if individuals are closely monitored and the dose increased at the onset of early signs of relapse, then the prophylactic impact of medication is not lost and there may be advantages in terms of improved medication adherence and fewer drug side-effects.

# Treatment resistance and the atypical neuroleptics

The last 10 years have witnessed the introduction of a new range of neuroleptics usually referred to as "atypical" neuroleptics, because of their unusual affinity for dopaminergic and 5-HT receptors (see Chapter 3).

One of these, the drug Risperidone, is atypical because it does not lead to side-effects at therapeutic doses (4–8mg per day) although akathesia is sometimes observed. Risperidone is better tolerated and has the advantage in one study at least of improved response for negative symptoms (Carman et al., 1995), although the benefits of reduced side-effects could be confused with negative symptoms and so the reduction in negative symptoms could be spurious (Marder, 2000). A further drug, Olanzapine, is also well tolerated but weight gain is common (Kane, 1999). It is clear, however, that these new atypical drugs do not have any additional antipsychotic potency compared with the traditional neuroleptics, but their advantage is confined to excellent tolerance in those for whom they are prescribed.

In recent years there has also been considerable excitement generated by a re-evaluation of the drug Clozapine, which is regarded as being particularly effective in cases of drug resistance, i.e., where the traditional neuroleptics have been unable to shift all psychotic symptoms. Studies have shown that up to two-thirds of patients with stubborn symptoms will respond positively within 12 months (Meltzer, 1999), although this figure is undoubtedly an overestimate since this includes many who are not strictly treatment resistant but who show intolerance to the traditional neuroleptics. Studies of the use of Clozapine in clinical practice suggest that perhaps a third of patients with severe drug-resistant symptoms will benefit significantly from the use of this drug (Meltzer, 1999). Clozapine is not a straightforward drug to use as it is associated with a potentially fatal lowering of the white blood count and so regular blood monitoring is a mandatory requirement of the licence; there are also reports of other side-effects including sedation, hypersalivation, and weight gain.

The atypical drugs, on the basis of these data alone, should be considered as a first-line treatment of psychotic symptoms in view of their favourable side-effects profile, but their high cost at the present time (which arises as a result of a major investment by the drug companies in research and development) is restricting their use. Also, it is not clear given the results of studies such as McEvoy et al. (1991) whether the atypicals really offer any advantage over low dose neuroleptic threshold pharmacotherapy for acute psychosis, in terms of clinical efficacy and side-effects.

# Summary

- There is little doubt that the neuroleptic drugs are effective in the treatment of distressing psychotic experiences. It is also clear that, since the introduction of the neuroleptics, there has been some improvement in the overall outcome for schizophrenia, though this is not quite as dramatic as has been supposed (Hegarty et al., 1994).
- The neuroleptic drugs offer a means of controlling, not curing, psychosis, and the data from the studies of Hogarty and colleagues show that they are particularly effective in delaying relapse rather than in preventing it. Relapse is still a high probability event among those individuals maintained on neuroleptics; perhaps up to 60% can expect an exacerbation within 2–3 years, and the prevalence of residual symptoms remains high.
- There is no convincing evidence that the neuroleptic drugs are effective for the negative symptoms, although the traditional preparations probably exacerbated them.
- The new generation of drugs does not show improved therapeutic efficacy but they are much better tolerated and are likely to show improved rates of adherence, although this has yet to be determined. It is important to underline that the prevention of relapse and the effective management of acute psychosis that the neuroleptic drugs offer are but a small part of the overall needs of people with psychosis.
- Even with optimum drug use, people continue to have multiple problems and disabilities associated with psychosis, and require a range of effective interventions at the social, psychological, and societal levels. We review these in the following two chapters.

# Social and community interventions 7

In this chapter we will consider those social and community interventions that can be used alone or in combination with medication to improve the quality of life for the person with psychosis.

## The therapeutic milieu

As discussed previously, in Chapter 2, a substantial body of evidence points to a major influence of social factors on the course of schizophrenia. In a now seminal study of the effects of ward atmosphere on social and clinical functioning, Wing and Brown (1970) studied three psychiatric hospitals, which differed with regard to ward environment and care offered. From each they drew a random sample of female inpatients with a diagnosis of schizophrenia who had been in hospital for 2 years or more. They were then rated on a number of measures such as positive and negative symptoms, behaviour on the ward, number of personal possessions, time spent off the ward, and time in social activities. Wing and Brown (1970) noted that there were significant differences in negative symptoms and behavioural ratings of withdrawal between those samples from hospitals where the ward environments were stimulating and those where they were not. This was later confirmed when the researchers returned to the hospitals 4 years later. After social changes at the poorest of the hospitals, major improvements in about a third of the patients were observed.

These results have been replicated across a number of community settings including day care (Linn, Caffey, Klett, Hogarty, & Lamb, 1979), hostel care (Hyde, Bridges, Goldberg et al., 1987), and community settings in general (Leff, Dayson, Gooch, Thornicroft, & Wills, 1996) and confirm that stimulating environments can significantly reduce negative symptoms and social withdrawal in schizophrenia. It is now widely accepted that normal life experience, provided it is not too stressful, is vital to promote self-esteem and a satisfactory quality of life.

## Social skills training

Interventions that focus on the interpersonal competence and social skills of people with schizophrenia have generally fallen under the rubric of "social skills training". Social impairments are often considered a major component of schizophrenia (Mueser, & Bellack, 1998) and poor social functioning is one of the criteria needed to make a diagnosis of schizophrenia (American Psychiatric Association, 1994). It was for such reasons that during the 1960s and 1970s a systematic attempt was made to develop interventions that would directly modify or improve the social behaviour of people with schizophrenia (Hersen & Bellack, 1976; Mueser, & Bellack, 1998).

One of the main assumptions underlying social skills training is that people with schizophrenia have either not learnt, or have forgotten, the behaviours necessary for successful social interactions and interpersonal relationships (Goldsmith, & McFool, 1975; Halford, & Hayes, 1992). Social skills training (SST) is a direct and active therapy that utilises a number of techniques and learning activities such as modelling, reinforcement, role playing, and *in vivo* practice in order to help patients to acquire the necessary verbal and nonverbal skills (Halford, & Hayes, 1992; Liberman, Spalding, & Corrigan, 1995). It is considered to be one of the most highly structured forms of psychosocial therapy for schizophrenia.

A typical social skills approach would be set up as an educational class with one or two trainers and five to ten patients as "students". Sessions last approximately 45–90 minutes and are held between one and five times a week (Liberman, De Risi, & Mueser, 1989). Topics covered may include: holding conversations, friendship making, conflict resolution, leisure and recreational activities, medication management, and vocational skills (Birchwood, & Spencer, 1999). Halford and Hayes (1992) have outlined a social skills training programme with examples of the modules that might be included, and this is shown in Table 7.1.

Each module focuses on a number of competencies in a key area of community functioning. For example, a conversational skills module will include ways of starting or opening up a conversation, the use of particular techniques such as open-ended questions, ways of

TABLE 7.1

**An example of the content of social skills training programme modules (from Halford & Hayes (1992) in Kavanagh, 1992)**

1. **Introduction**
   Introduction of group members
   Feedback of assessment data
   Negotiating individual goals

2. **Conversation skills**
   Starting a conversation
   Using open-ended questions and expanded replies
   Generating conversation content
   Nonverbal communication
   Ending a conversation

3. **Assertion and conflict management**
   Discrimination of assertion
   Nonassertion and aggression
   Negative assertion
   Conflict resolution
   Positive assertion
   Empathic assertion

4. **Medication self-management**
   Knowledge of medication
   Self-monitoring of medication
   Knowledge of symptoms and side-effects
   Self-monitoring and management of symptoms and side-effects
   Discussing symptoms and medication with health professionals
   Relapse warning sign identification

5. **Time use and recreational skills**
   Assessment of time use and recreational activity
   Identification of recreational activities to increase
   Using the telephone to obtain information
   Gathering information on recreation
   Planning the use of free time

6. **Survival skills**
   Budgeting and money management
   Banking
   Seeking and establishing accommodation
   Knowledge of and interaction with community resources and welfare agencies

7. **Employment skills**
   Job-seeking strategies
   Gathering information on jobs
   Interview skills
   Job maintenance skills

generating conversation content, interpretation and translation of nonverbal gestures, and how to end a conversation. Thus, each competency is composed of the specific knowledge and skills required for that competency (Liberman et al., 1995).

Studies evaluating SST for people with schizophrenia have been reviewed elsewhere (Birchwood, & Spencer, 1999). These reviews conclude that SST is effective in increasing patients' ability, comfort, and assertiveness in social situations (Birchwood, & Spencer, 1999). However, one of the early criticisms of SST was that the training did not generalise to "real life" and was not durable (Hemsley, 1993b). For instance, Shepherd (1977) failed to find any improvements in interactional skills following an SST programme when he assessed the social functioning of patients across a number of naturalistic settings, using independent observers. Although, as improvements to training programmes have been made with particular emphasis upon training those skills which are most relevant to everyday life, more favourable results have been reported. Reports of patients maintaining skills for more than 2 years are not uncommon (Kindness, & Newton, 1984), although it is still likely that deterioration in social skills will occur if active intervention is not maintained (Hogarty, Anderson, Reiss et al., 1991).

The last few years have seen a change in the emphasis placed upon the learning of social skills as a discrete set of "micro-skills", which when combined produce competent social behaviour (Morrison, & Bellack, 1984). Nowadays theories emphasise deficits in social information processing (Corrigan, & Green, 1993; Liberman et al., 1995; Trower, Bryant, & Argyle, 1978). For instance, Donohoe, Carter, Bloem, and Wallace (1991) noted that people with schizophrenia demonstrated diminished ability to understand interpersonal problems and initiate adequate solutions. Thus, it is likely that adequate social behaviour not only requires behavioural skills, but also cognitive and social perception skills (Mueser, & Bellack, 1998) and that if an intervention is to be effective, it would also need to address these areas (i.e., teaching social perception skills).

## Vocational training and rehabilitation

In developed countries, the vast majority of people with schizophrenia are unemployed. It is estimated, for instance, that only 25–30% of schizophrenic patients return to work within 6 months of their discharge from hospital, and only half of these are still employed 1 year later (Glynn, & MacKain, 1992). This is especially true for those with chronic psychosis or those with particularly severe negative symptoms. Yet employment status may have a significant impact upon how well someone recovers from schizophrenia (Warner, 1994), whether their symptoms worsen (Hagen, 1983), and on their general quality of life (Priebe, Warner, Hubschmid, & Eckle, 1998). In order to help people with schizophrenia get back to work, a number of programmes have been developed.

## Supported employment

Supported employment is based on the idea that individuals will be more employable if they are matched with an existing job in the local economy and provided with the appropriate training on site rather than given long training periods in preparatory and prevocational settings (Anthony, & Blanch, 1987). This is sometimes referred to as "place and train" and the idea was originally devised to help find employment for people with learning disabilities. Each person is assigned a "job coach" whose duty it is to ensure that the person with mental illness is productively involved at the work site.

A major component of supported employment is the provision of support and guidance (Liberman et al., 1995). Placements may be permanent or limited to a few months. Although jobs are often found in both large and small businesses, they are usually unskilled positions such as messengers, clerks, or kitchen helpers (Glasscote, Cumming, & Rutman, 1979). There are advantages for employers, which include reduced job recruitment, turnover, and training costs, as well as assurance of reliability from the agency providing the employee.

Supported employment schemes for people with schizophrenia are in their infancy and as such still need to be properly evaluated. There is some evidence that about 75% of those taking part in supportive employment work continuously for 3 months, and approximately half of all participants will be working in community placements at the end of the first year (Bond, Drake, Mueser, & Becker, 1997).

## Job clubs

Another popular innovation is the job-finding club. This was initially set up as a means of providing people with a wide range of mental health difficulties the basic skills needed to find and apply for jobs, prepare for interviews, and other aspects of gaining appropriate employment. The club acts as a resource centre during the job-seeking phase by providing telephones, maps, and support. The benefits of job clubs for people with schizophrenia have, on the whole, not mirrored the initial success found for people with emotional or substance abuse disorders (Eisenberg, & Cole, 1986). However, there is evidence that once people with schizophrenia are successful in obtaining employment, they are as likely as any other diagnostic group to keep their jobs (i.e., 68% for a period of at least 6 months; Jacobs et al., 1990).

## Community care

Between 1955 and 1991, the number of hospital beds for the mentally ill was reduced from 560,000 to 100,000 in the United States and from 155,000 to 59,000 in the UK (Muijen, & Hadley, 1995). Throughout the developed world there has been a wholesale shift towards managing and treating people with schizophrenia in the community. To a large extent, community care has replaced official hospital care for this group of people. The reasons for such a change in service provision are numerous and complex, but include political, economic, and clinical factors (Lavender, & Holloway, 1992).

Throughout the 1960s and 1970s the growing "antipsychiatry" movement, encouraged by the writings of such people as Szasz and Laing, began to reject medical concepts of mental illness. Psychotherapy and support in community settings were given preference over medication (Lavender, & Holloway, 1992; Sedgwick, 1982) and other physical treatments. At the same time research was emerging that fuelled the idea that institutional psychiatric hospitals may in some way be detrimental to the outcomes of people with schizophrenia. Such places were criticised on the grounds that they were de-humanising and increased negative symptoms and a wide range of other physical and mental disabilities (Wing, & Brown, 1970).

The discovery of the neuroleptic drugs also allowed psychiatrists to move from psychiatric hospitals into district general hospitals and to expand outpatient day care for schizophrenia (Brown, Bone, Dalison, & Wing, 1966; Scull, 1983). Politically, such changes were seized upon in both the US and the UK and seen as a possible solution to an ongoing crisis in the funding of the welfare state.

Community care was, erroneously, considered to be a cheaper alternative to hospital.

Community care has both its critics and its protagonists. The protagonists argue that the quality of life for people with schizophrenia can be improved by treating them at home, with only minimal reliance on psychiatric hospitals and at no extra cost to the taxpayer (Muijen, & Hadley, 1995). Hospitals are seen as places that: medicalise psychosocial problems; increase not decrease disabilities associated with schizophrenia, such as apathy, withdrawal, and anhedonia; provide abnormal environments, which make it difficult to develop useful social and living skills for where they are most likely to be applied (i.e., in the community); and stigmatise those with mental illness (Hoult, & Reynolds, 1983; Muijen, & Hadley, 1995).

Critics of community care, on the other hand, argue that services are often patchy and not well developed (see Muijen, 1992, for a review) and tend to overlook particularly vulnerable groups such as those from long-stay wards (who have spent a significant proportion of their life in hospitals) and young people with inadequate emotional and social support who often do not fit neatly into any of the newly established community services (Birchwood, Fowler, & Jackson, 2000; McGorry, & Jackson, 1999). People with schizophrenia and drug and alcohol problems (so-called dual diagnosis) may also fall between different services (Drake, Brunette, & Mueser, 1998; Pepper, Kirschner, & Rylewics, 1981). Some clinicians and workers in the field have argued that, because of inadequate provision, people become institutionalised in other community settings such as hostels and prisons, that the burden upon families is increased, and that staff are deprofessionalised (Bassuk, & Gerson, 1978; Hawks, 1975; Weller, 1989).

The media in the UK and the USA have criticised community care with high profile reports of tragic cases such as that of Christopher Clunis who murdered Jonathan Zito, a stranger, on an underground station in London. Conclusions from public enquiries into such cases have placed emphasis upon the failings of community care policy. The more dispassionate view, however, is that such failings are not so much to do with the principles and ideologies of a community care policy but how it has been delivered, executed, and, ultimately, how it has been resourced (Muijen, & Hadley, 1995).

## Models of community care

Until recently, and for much of the last 30 years, a so-called acute care or "throughput" model has dominated the psychiatric treatment of schizophrenia (Craig, 1998). In essence, this model has been built on the premise that if one treats acute episodes of psychosis vigorously and as a crisis, one can then discharge people back to their GP or a primary care agency for monitoring until their next acute episode. Such an approach has been defended on the grounds that it works well in other branches of medicine and allows expert and professional medical help to be suitably rationed to those times when it is most needed (Craig, 1998). In contrast, the continuing care model places more emphasis on ongoing interventions *between* psychotic episodes in order to maintain the benefits of acute treatment and prevent relapse and deterioration. "Case management" is considered an essential element of the community care model.

Case management is a way of "tailoring help to meet individual need by placing the responsibility for assessment and service coordination with one individual worker or team" (Onyett, 1992). It generally relies on a long-term relationship between clients and their professional carers. In most cases, a client will be allocated to a named keyworker or case manager (usually a community psychiatric nurse [CPN] or social worker) whose job it is to assess and coordinate the appropriate care required to meet that person's ongoing needs. This may require the input from a number of other agencies (social services, housing, co-ops, employment agencies) or professionals (psychologists, occupational therapists, etc.). In practice there is great variation in how case management models are delivered through community teams (Mueser, Bond, Drake, & Resnick, 1998). To capture such variations in the practice of case management, Robinson, Bergman, and Scallet (1989) described four models: (1) the *expanded broker model*, placing emphasis on case managers facilitating contacts between patients and appropriate care services; (2) the *personal strengths model*, focusing on enhancing the abilities and strengths of the individual client via an "advocacy–mentor" approach; (3) the *rehabilitation approach*, based on the notion that skill acquisition can be taught within a client/therapist relationship in order to improve living skills; and (4) the *assertive community treatment model* (ACT), perhaps the best known of all the case management models, and one based on the provision of medical, social, and psychological interventions through a more paternalistic, directed approach.

The ACT model, when applied to intervening with people with schizophrenia, usually requires a specialist team made up of psychologists, occupational therapists, social workers, psychiatrists, and community psychiatric nurses. Shepherd (1998) has claimed such teams should be clearly targeted with small caseloads of between 10 and 15 clients per case manager, have "extended hours" of operation (i.e., outside Monday to Friday, 9–5pm), with an emphasis upon flexibility, availability (i.e., "on tap" but not "on top"), and continuity (Jackson, & Farmer, 1998).

As the focus of psychiatric care has moved from hospital into the community, there have been a number of attempts to evaluate the impact of the community-based treatment programmes on the lives of people with schizophrenia when compared with standard inpatient care. A study by Stein and Test (1980) is still generally regarded as a benchmark study against which others are compared because of the quality of their community programme and research design. They compared two groups of 65 individuals, one receiving in-patient care plus aftercare, the other receiving "training in community living". This included: the availability of material resources (food, shelter, and so on); training in basic community survival skills; developing social-support networks; reducing dependency of family or institutions by promoting autonomy and involvement in wider community life; and support and education of community members who were involved with the individual (for example, hostel workers, families, and so on). The results of the programme were highly impressive: during the first 12 months of the study, 12 out of 65 experimental subjects were readmitted, compared with 58 out of 65 controls, with equally favourable outcome in terms of social functioning and residual symptoms. However, when the programme ended, the gains were steadily lost. Those in the community programme were not "cured": many continued to experience symptoms and were functioning at a socially marginal level. Marks, Connolly, and Muijen (1988) suggested that a reduced need for readmission came about as a result of the "availability to supporters and carers of a twenty four hour emergency service which even though little used, the knowledge that it could be . . . prevented readmission" (p. 22). Similar results have been reported in parallel investigations in Australia (Hoult, & Reynolds, 1983) and other parts of North America (Fenton, Tessier, Struening, Smith, & Benoit, 1982).

One of the major advantages of the community outreach approach has been its ability to engage and maintain contact with often difficult and challenging clients. Loss of contact can very occasionally have disastrous consequences for the client and/or others (Ritchie et al., 1994).

# Summary

- Social and community interventions have often been used in combination with medical and psychological treatments to improve the outcomes of people with schizophrenia.
- Social skills training (SST) is a systematic attempt to help people with schizophrenia improve their interpersonal and social behaviours.
- Helping people with schizophrenia back to work remains a high priority for which a number of initiatives have been developed.
- There has been a shift away from treating people with schizophrenia in hospital towards more community-based approaches.
- A number of community-based treatment programmes have been developed, particularly assertive community treatment, and evaluated, with generally positive outcomes.

# Psychosocial interventions 8

There has been a considerable advance in the psychological treatment of schizophrenia in recent years. These advances have been informed by an improved understanding of the relationship between stress and psychology (see Chapter 4) and how the person with psychosis can in spite of their illness develop a degree of control over their symptoms. In this chapter we will discuss psychological interventions which fall into four broad areas: "cognitive-behavioural" strategies, cognitive therapy, relapse prevention work, and family intervention.

## Cognitive-behavioural strategies

Cognitive-behavioural interventions in schizophrenia have focused mainly upon individual symptoms, particularly hallucinations and delusions. Early efforts adopted a "behavioural" approach focusing on the behaviours that were thought to be concomitant with the experience of symptoms (e.g., shouting at voices). These approaches used behavioural techniques to control such anomalous behaviour and were, by and large, based on single case or small group studies and their findings largely negative. These approaches were somewhat naive in assuming that modifying behaviour alone would reduce the distress and problems associated with psychotic experience (Birchwood, & Preston, 1991). In fact, it is the experience of distress associated with positive psychotic symptoms that underpins anomalous behaviour, particularly anxiety and depression, and also, in the case of persecutory delusions, anger and indignation (Birchwood, & Chadwick, 1997).

The presence of such intense distress would be expected to produce efforts to alleviate it, and studies conducted in the 1980s demonstrated that people troubled by psychotic symptoms do indeed engage in a variety of coping strategies to eliminate unpleasant distress but also in response to the threat posed by supposed persecutors. Breier and Strauss (1983) were among the first to show that the presence of a major psychotic experience does not prevent the individual from using strategies for coping and that, once the individual's perspective is understood, in many ways their strategies appear rational and coherent. For example, individuals who feel threatened by a malevolent persecutor may make attempts to reduce the threat by seeking out those who they feel may be responsible or by engaging in active surveillance of their immediate environment to detect and deter potential danger.

Breier and Strauss (1983) also noted that many individuals continued to experience psychotic symptoms and yet maintained some awareness that these beliefs could be the result of illness and adopted strategies that distracted their attention away from them. Falloon and Talbot (1981) conducted a seminal investigation of the coping strategies of people who hear voices and found that over three-quarters of their sample reported such strategies, which they used with the explicit intention of easing distress. They did not find that any particular strategy was associated with reduced stress but concluded that the availability of at least one strategy, perceived by the individual to be helpful and implemented regularly, was associated with a sense of well-being and a sense of control over the psychotic experience.

Nick Tarrier (1987) from Manchester in the UK has pursued this approach with considerable sophistication. He reported the use of coping strategies in 25 patients who were identified as experiencing hallucinations and/or delusions during a 9-month period following an acute episode of psychosis. Using a detailed interview, individuals' accounts of their psychotic experiences were elicited, as were the situations in which these experiences were likely to occur, their emotional reactions, and their use of coping strategies. He noted that approximately one-third of his sample were able to identify antecedents or "triggers" to the symptoms, which varied from specific stimuli such as traffic noise, television, social situations, to emotional states such as feeling anxious. Three-quarters reported major distress and one-third indicated that these symptoms disrupted their thinking and ongoing behaviour; again, three-quarters disclosed the use of coping strategies. Cognitive strategies were used by approximately 40%, including the use of distraction, "attention narrowing" (e.g., focusing or concentrating on a particular task), and positive self-talk. One-third of patients used behavioural strategies including initiation of social contact, and 25% either withdrew or engaged in solitary activities. Other strategies included the use of relaxation or breathing exercises and attempts to "drown out" voices by, for example, turning up the volume on the television. Consistent with previous studies, 72% reported at least one of their strategies to be moderately successful in controlling their symptoms. Importantly, it was found that using multiple coping strategies, thus giving them a range of options for coping, was associated with their perceived effectiveness in coping with symptoms.

These studies informed the development of a new therapeutic approach, which involved teaching patients new coping strategies building upon those that they themselves had found useful. This approach was termed Coping Strategy Enhancement (CSE). The aim of CSE is systematically to teach the individual the use of effective coping strategies to reduce the frequency, intensity, and duration of the psychotic symptoms together with the accompanying distress. Careful assessment is the key to CSE and involves assessing the form and the content of the psychotic experience, the accompanying emotional response (for example, anxiety, fear, anger), together with the thoughts or cognitions that accompany these emotions, for example beliefs about danger or of hopelessness. The individual is asked about the occurrence of any antecedent or precipitating context for each symptom (e.g., "Can you tell me when the voice is going to occur?", "How do you know?", "When are your concerns about persecution most intense?"). The individuals' coping strategies are again carefully elicited through interview, using common probes ("How do you cope with this?", "How do you make yourself feel better?", "Is there anything you can do to get rid of the voice?"). Strategies to ease distress are also elicited, for example: "Is there anything you can do to help yourself by feeling a certain way such as relaxing?", or "Can you help yourself by thinking in a certain way, or telling yourself certain things?" When the repertoire of coping strategies has been established, the individual is asked to rate each strategy in terms of its effectiveness, for example as moderate or very effective. The aim of CSE is to systematically teach the patient the use of effective strategies, building upon the presence of existing useful strategies, and encouraging the individual to experiment with strategies adopted by other patients. CSE involves two components. (1) *Education and rapport training*: this involves developing a shared understanding and an atmosphere in which the therapist and client can work together to improve the effectiveness of the individual's repertoire of coping strategies; this is sometimes known as "collaborative empiricism". Providing the individual with information about schizophrenia may be used. (2) *Symptom targeting*: a target symptom is selected, often on the basis of one for which the individual already has developed some effective coping strategies. These coping strategies may be enhanced by, for example, increasing their range of application. Where appropriate, the new coping strategy will be introduced and practised within a session, carefully monitoring any problems the individual encounters in using it. The individual is then asked to monitor its effectiveness, is given "homework" tasks to implement the strategy in a particular situation at a particular time, and is asked to record the implementation of the strategy. The individual might be given further "booster" practice and further encouragement to implement it in real-life settings. Crucial to CSE is the adoption of at least two strategies for each symptom based on Tarrier's finding that the presence of coping options is associated with reduced distress.

A controlled trial has been reported evaluating the CSE approach with patients with a diagnosis of schizophrenia living in the community who continue to experience distressing hallucinations or delusions in spite of antipsychotic medication (Tarrier, Beckett, Harwood et al., 1993). The CSE method was compared with "problem-solving therapy", which was selected as a control treatment as it is an established cognitive-behavioural treatment method used in a variety of psychological problems. Forty-nine patients were entered into the trial; however, 45% of these either refused to participate or dropped out, which is a problem that bedevils this and other forms of treatment research in schizophrenia. Twenty-seven continued to receive treatment and were followed up 6 months later. Patients were randomly allocated to the treatment conditions, which involved ten, 1-hour sessions. The results demonstrated that patients in both treatment conditions obtained significant improvements in positive symptoms compared with those who were on a "waiting list" for the treatment. Although the differences between CSE and the control treatment were marginal, the overall treatment gains were maintained at 6 months follow-up. Tarrier et al. report that over 50% of patients demonstrated a significant decrease in hallucinations and/or delusions. Patients receiving CSE showed a significant improvement in coping skills, which were in turn associated with a decrease in hallucinations and delusions. Patients in the problem-solving condition did not show improvements in coping skills. This important study represents one of the first studies of cognitive-behavioural therapy and has inspired further work including a large-scale replication trial.

# Cognitive therapy

Cognitive therapy comes from the same stable as cognitive-behavioural therapy but is exclusively focused on beliefs and ongoing patterns of thinking. It is an approach that is rooted in the work of Albert Ellis and of Aaron Beck in the USA and has been developed with considerable specification as an effective therapy for depression and for panic disorder (Hammen, 1997; Rachman, 1998). This approach argues that it is beliefs about the self, and appraisals of events, that are directly responsible for generating or maintaining distress or other negative affect. It involves a systematic method of eliciting thoughts and their associated affect and of challenging the beliefs in a systematic way, which might involve putting such beliefs to an empirical or reality test. This approach has been developed again with considerable sophistication by a number of groups in the UK including Fowler and colleagues (1995), Kingdon and Turkington (1994) and Chadwick, Birchwood, and Trower (1996).

As in CSE, the process of engagement and rapport building is critical to the successful implementation of cognitive therapy. The patient must feel that they are engaged in a genuine collaborative process in which the therapist takes the patient's beliefs and concerns seriously and engages in a collaborative endeavour to determine the veracity or otherwise of the beliefs with the prime aim of reducing distress. The beliefs that are the subject of cognitive therapy always include the delusional beliefs (including beliefs about voices) that are directly responsible for the individual's distress but also other beliefs, for example about the individual's self-worth. The client must share this spirit of collaboration and feel that he or she is not to be humiliated should a change of belief emerge. It is important to bear in mind that this approach to reasoning with delusions was regarded for many years as impossible, if not potentially harmful to patients' well-being. Watts, Powell, and Austin (1973) argued that a danger when trying to modify delusions, indeed, all strongly held beliefs, is "psychological reactance"; whereby too direct an approach served only to reinforce the belief. Two principles that Watts et al. offered to minimise this possibility were to begin with the least important belief, and also to work with the evidence for the belief rather than the belief itself.

Accordingly, a "verbal challenge" of delusions begins by questioning the evidence for the belief, and this process begins with the least significant item and works up to the most significant. The preferred approach is that with each item of evidence the therapist questions the client's delusional interpretation and puts forward a more reasonable and probable one. The customary approach in cognitive therapy is for the client to be asked to generate the alternative interpretation(s), rather than for the therapist to supply one.

When the therapist questions the evidence for a delusion he or she has in mind two distant but related objectives. One is to encourage the client to question and perhaps even to reject the evidence for his or her belief, and in this way perhaps to undermine the client's conviction in the delusion itself. For some individuals, challenging the evidence is a very powerful intervention and one that produces a substantial reduction in delusional conviction. However, more commonly this does not happen, but challenging the evidence is still valuable in that it does impart insight into the connection between events, beliefs, affect, and behaviour. This is the second objective of challenging evidence, to convey the essentials of the cognitive approach—that is, that strongly held beliefs influence behaviour, affect, and interpretation for all people.

## Inconsistency and irrationality

Although delusions contain differing degrees of inconsistency and irrationality, they all seem to contain some. However, we should not feel too smug because it appears that few complex belief systems are watertight; what at times can be surprising is the enormity of the inconsistency. Anne held two delusions, formed at different points in her life, which were actually mutually exclusive. One was that she was only a teenager and that the life experience she thought had been hers was fed in using "fancy computers and autosuggestion"; another belief was that during her life (i.e., the one she recalled as hers, which the first delusion wiped out) she had been raped numerous times and had six children, each following a pregnancy of six days. It is possible to weaken what was a towering delusional edifice by using the more important delusion to eradicate the other altogether.

## Empirical testing

It is an integral part of cognitive therapy that the belief or assumption under consideration be put to empirical test. "Reality testing", as it is known, involves planning and performing an activity, which validates or invalidates a belief, or part of a belief. This includes:

1. Specify the inference the test is assessing (if . . . then . . .).
2. Review existing evidence for the predicted outcome.
3. Devise a specific experiment to test the validity of the prediction.
4. Note and learn from the results.
5. Draw conclusions from this specific test.

When working with delusions, a clear alternative belief is set up in opposition to the delusion and the hospital clarifies with the client in advance precisely what has to happen for each to be supported and refuted.

For example, Nigel claimed to have special powers, including being able to know what people were going to say before they said it and being able to make things happen by simply thinking it (see Chadwick, Birchwood, & Trower, 1996). Nigel thought the people might have something to do with God. He reported having held the belief for 3 years and having never doubted it. He was preoccupied by the belief four or five times a day; at these times he felt some sadness and anxiety. On one occasion he said that the power made him want to kill himself because it was interfering so much in his life, in particular his enjoyment of television was spoilt by his sense of knowing what was about to be said, and, indeed, he would sometimes not bother watching. Also, it gave him a sense of certainty at the betting shop, which his winnings did not justify! The test with Nigel was straightforward and was initially suggested by him as a way of proving his power. Several different video recorders were put on pause at prearranged times, and he was then asked to say what was coming up next. In practice, Nigel did not get a single one right, out of over 50, and he concluded that he did not have the power at all.

## Research evidence

A number of research trials of this method have been reported. They have demonstrated a 40% reduction in the severity of psychotic symptoms of people with longstanding illness (Kuipers, Garety, Fowler et al., 1997) and, when used at a time of acute psychosis, cognitive therapy led to a faster response to treatment compared with drugs alone, and to improved recovery (Drury et al., 1996).

# Early intervention in relapse

Prospective studies of relapse in psychosis have suggested that relapse is not a discrete phenomenon but a *process* in which patients respond to initially subtle changes in mental functioning, including attention dysfunction, perceptual distortions, and racing thoughts, which develop into symptoms such as dysphoria (anxiety, withdrawal, restlessness) and early psychotic symptoms (including suspiciousness, ideas of reference, misinterpretations) over a period of between 1 and 3 weeks (Birchwood et al., 1989; Herz, & Melville, 1980; Subotnik, & Nuechterlein, 1988). These studies reveal that "prodromes", or "early warning signs", precede relapse in two-thirds of instances; that there can be "false alarms" in up to 20% of cases; and that each person has their own personalised set of early symptoms, or a "relapse signature" (Birchwood, MacMillan, & Smith, 1989).

## Prodromes: Discrete or continuous?

The prospective studies have rather assumed, however, that prodromal and psychotic symptoms are dichotomous stages that may each be scored as present or absent. The notion of "prodrome" is, of course, taken from general medicine where nonspecific symptoms (e.g., malaise) precede the illness proper (e.g., AIDS). In fact, most of the prospective studies do not maintain such a clear distinction: Tarrier et al. (1993) included a scale of "incipient psychosis" with items indicating low-level psychotic signs ("something odd is going on which cannot be explained"; "feeling people are taking unusual notice of me"). Subotnik and Nuechterlein (1988) included BPRS "thought disturbance" in their prodrome, which is, of course, not strictly a nonpsychotic symptom. Malla and Norman (1994), using only nonpsychotic symptom measures, found no link between prodromes and psychosis, where both are viewed as continuous, but they did find that major increases in psychosis were preceded by nonpsychotic signs, although the sensitivity was lower than that found in the other prospective studies. Even the status of dysphoria as a nonspecific prodromal symptom is contentious since there is sound evidence that dysphasia accompanies acute psychosis and depression features as a dimension of psychopathology in some of the duties of the structure of psychotic symptoms. Also, in some formulations, dysphasia is regarded as a reaction to a developing psychosis rather than a prodrome proper (Birchwood et al., 1992; see later).

## The concept of the relapse signature

The prospective studies have raised a number of questions. They have confirmed the existence of prodromes of psychotic relapse and find a true positive rate in the region of 50–60%, with a false positive rate of up to 25%; however, their limitations have not enabled a clear picture to emerge of the true predictive significance of apparent early warning signs. If the concept of the relapse signature is borne out, then group studies in the mould of Subotnik and Nuechterlein (1988) would be inherently limited, as they could not capture the apparent qualitative differences *between* patients in their early signs or symptoms. This is supported by Subotnik and Neuchterlein's finding that greater prediction came when patients were compared against their own baseline, rather than that of other patients. It may be more appropriate to think of each patient's syndrome as a personalised *relapse signature*, which includes core or common symptoms together with features unique to each patient. If an individual's relapse signature can be identified, then it might be expected that the overall power of "prodromal" symptoms can be achieved only once further information becomes available to build a more accurate image of the signature. This kind of learning process had been acknowledged by patients (Breier & Strauss, 1983) and could be adapted and developed by professionals and carers; it forms the basis of our (Birchwood et al., 1992) approach to early intervention.

## Engagement and education

Early intervention rests on a close collaboration between patient, carer/relative, and professionals. Education about prodromes and early intervention opportunities need to be provided, which might be given in the context of general educational intervention about psychosis (Birchwood et al., 1992; Smith, & Birchwood, 1990). Education must emphasise that responsibility is being placed on the individual and relative to recognise a potential relapse and to initiate treatment. Engagement and compliance will be enhanced where the client has a stable, trusting relationship with individuals in the mental health services. As the experience of Jolley, Hirsch, Morrison et al. (1990) illustrated, this requires psycho-education to be a continuous feature of this relationship. The continuity of care inherent in the case management approach provides an appropriate support structure.

## Identifying the time window and "relapse signature" for early intervention

Four prodromes need to be overcome if our knowledge about the process of relapse is to have clinical application. (1) The identification of "early signs" by a clinician would require intensive, regular monitoring of mental state at least fortnightly, which is rarely possible in clinical practice. (2) Some patients choose to conceal their symptoms as relapse approaches and insight declines (Heinrichs, & Carpenter, 1985). (3) Many patients experience persisting symptoms, cognitive defects, or drug side-effects, which may obscure the visibility of the prodromes. Indeed, the nature of a prodrome in patients with residual symptoms (in contrast to those who are symptom-free) has not been studied, and is important, since in clinical practice the pressure of residual symptoms is extremely common. (4) The possibility is raised that the characteristics of prodromes might vary from individual to individual and this information may be lost in scales of general psychopathology.

With regard to the latter, precise information about the nature and duration of an individual's prodrome or "relapse signature" may be obtained through careful interviewing of the patient (and, if possible, relatives and other close associates) about the changes in thinking and behaviour leading up to a recent episode. Where this is fed back, it may enable a more accurate discrimination of a future prodrome.

## Intervention

In the next stage, decision rules are discerned to define the onset of a prodrome operationally; these may include a quantitative change on a stabilised scale (e.g., the Early Signs Scale [ESS]; Birchwood et al., 1989) and/or the appearance of indiviualised prodromal signs. This, then, is an entirely patient-driven and controlled system as is the intervention. Once a prodrome has been declared, the individual and family need intensive support. The psychological reaction to a loss of well-being and the possibility that this may herald a relapse places a significant strain on both parties, which, if unchecked, could accelerate deterioration. The availability of support, quick access to the team, and the use of stress management, diversionary activities, and medication may help to mitigate these effects (Breier & Strauss, 1983), and checking the development of the procedure weekly, daily, or even inpatient contact can be offered, serving to alleviate anxiety and emphasising the shared burden of responsibility. Impending or actual crises present an important opportunity to "sharpen the image" of the signature for patient, carer, and professionals; in this respect the crises can be reframed as an opportunity to acquire information that can facilitate control and prevention.

## Research evidence

Most of the research paradigms have involved withdrawing patients from maintenance medication, monitoring clinical state, and providing brief pharmacotherapy at the onset of a "prodrome". This paradigm has been chosen with the goal of minimising drug exposure and therefore side-effects, without increasing relapse risk, rather than as a means of controlling further relapse. Three well-controlled studies have been reported using this paradigm. Jolley et al. (1990) studied 54 stabilised, symptomatic, and thus highly selected patients, who were randomly assigned to active or placebo maintenance therapy conditions, with both receiving targeted drug interventions at the onset of a prodrome involving the administration of 5–10mg daily of Haloperidol. Patients received a brief educational session on entry to the study (about prodromes and early intervention) as reliance was placed on patients to recognise their early signs of relapse and to contact the clinical team. Outcome at 1 year revealed that significantly more patients experienced prodromal symptoms in the intermittent group (over 30% vs 7%), although there was good evidence that severe relapse was not affected and was indeed low in both groups. Nevertheless, the large difference between the number of prodromes and number of relapses suggested that prompt action can abort relapse in many instances. During the first year of the study, 73% of relapses were preceded by identified prodromal symptoms; during the second year this fell to 25%, as reliance was placed on patients and families to identify and seek assistance for prodromal symptoms. This suggests "that the single teaching session at the start of the study does not provide patients and families with an adequate grasp of the intermittent paradigm . . . ongoing psycho-education should be an essential component of further studies" (Jolley et al., 1990, p. 841).

Carpenter, Hanlon, Heinrichs, et al. (1990) report the outcome of a study of similar design to that of Jolley and colleagues, with largely similar outcomes. However, in their study, not only was the intermittent regime less effective, it was less popular too: 50% refused to continue with the regime (vs 20% in continuous treatment), presumably due to higher rate of prodromes and hospitalisations and perhaps also due to the fact that patients found the responsibility placed on them to recognise relapse an excessive one.

Gaebel et al. (1993) report a multicentre German open trial comparing maintenance and targeted medication, targeted medication alone ("early intervention") and no pharmacotherapy. Six "prodromal" symptoms were measured by the participating psychiatrists on a regular basis; impending relapse was decided on the basis of a "significant increase" in these symptoms, but was essentially determined by the psychiatrist. The study found that relapse under targeted pharmacotherapy alone (49%) was less than no pharmacotherapy (63%) but was greater than maintenance and targeted pharmacotherapy combined (23%). This study suffered from a massive drop-out of over 56%, similar to the Carpenter study, and no data are presented regarding selectivity of drop-outs by experimental condition. Unlike the other studies, the results do suggest that targeted medication alone is effective in controlling relapse compared with no treatment, but again the value and relative popularity of maintenance medication is clearly underlined. Marder et al. (1984, 1987) studied patients assigned to a low (5mg) or standard (20mg) dose maintenance regime of Fluphenazine Decanoate over 2 weeks and at the first sign of exacerbation the dose was doubled. If this failed patients were considered to have relapsed, which occurred in 22% taking the lower doses and in 20% on the higher dose, with fewer side-effects in the former. Marder et al. found that lower doses carried a greater risk of relapse, but these were not "serious" and were eliminated once the clinician was permitted to double the dose at the onset of a prodrome (the survival curves of the dosage groups were no different under targeted conditions). This was later followed up by a study of low dose neuroleptic maintenance treatment in schizophrenia (Marder et al., 1994) in which 36 patients were given additional medication (10mg of Fluphenazine Hydrochloride) under double-blind conditions following the appearance of operationally defined "prodromes". Prodromal symptoms were monitored weekly in each group using an individually tailored "idiosyncratic prodromal scale", including the three most common symptoms arising from the baseline interviews with each patient and an informant, similar to the methodology outlined by Birchwood et al. (1989). Analyses beginning at the start of the second year demonstrated a significant reduction in relapse risk for those receiving active drug supplementation, who spent less time in psychosis during the second year.

In conclusion, early intervention in the process of relapse has been shown to be an effective procedure when implemented in the context of regular maintenance medication; importantly, it is an approach that involves the patient directly in monitoring and controlling his or her illness, a theme running through many of the advances in psychological therapy covered in this chapter.

# Family intervention

The literature on expressed emotion (EE) described in Chapter 4 has demonstrated that certain characteristics of family life indicative of stressful or strained relationships between the patient and key relative have been shown to be robust predictors of relapse. These data have inspired a number of family intervention programmes designed with the specific aim of reducing the rate of relapse among families characterised by high expressed emotion. These interventions are usually offered in addition to neuroleptic medication and share a number of common features, which appear to be crucial for their effectiveness.

First of all, much attention is paid at the start to establish a collaborative working relationship with all family members including the person with schizophrenia. A positive nonblaming attitude on the part of the therapist helps to establish a working alliance where the family and therapist together attempt to find new ways of coping and effective solutions to problems faced. There is always an emphasis on sharing of information about the disorder, and topics such as the cause, prognosis, symptoms, and treatments are presented. While the therapist brings his or her knowledge to the therapy so too do the family members, and the person who has experienced a psychotic episode is often seen as an "expert" on the disorder. Sessions usually involve both the person with schizophrenia and the family members. The orientation of the intervention includes a core emphasis on finding practical solutions to day-to-day problems. The therapy aims to assist family members in acquiring a range of coping skills that will help them to deal with the difficulties they have to face as a consequence of one of the family members having a serious mental disorder. Usually this starts off by addressing simple or straightforward difficulties and may include topics involved in the day-to-day life of households such as household tasks, planning activities together, and so on. At a later stage more emotive topics such as the management of distressing behaviour (e.g., how to cope with expression of a paranoid delusion) and also relatives' own needs are addressed; the latter can often be sacrificed in the difficult challenge of supporting someone with a serious mental illness such as schizophrenia.

There is often an emphasis on communication in an attempt to help family members learn more constructive ways of interacting with one another. The acknowledgement that the atmosphere in the household may have become negative or concentrated solely on difficulties often leads to a focus on developing more positive ways of communicating. This might include paying attention to the good things that happen, making requests of each other in a direct and clear way, rather than, for example, using communication patterns that involve demanding, nagging, or being sarcastic. At the same time it is acknowledged that there are some feelings within the family such as anger, irritation, and disappointment that can be difficult to express. Families are encouraged to find ways of expressing these feelings in order to reduce the likelihood of using them excessively. These skills are usually practised within sessions and family members and therapists make suggestions and give feedback to one another on potential changes or alternative ways of coping. In addition, all family members are encouraged to have their own interests and goals that they would like to achieve. This may include maintaining social contacts, personal interests, and giving individuals a break from one another in the family. The family and the individual are also taught to recognise the early warning signs of relapse and to engage with services at a very early point to avert crisis.

## Outcome studies

A number of studies evaluating family intervention have been conducted, which are summarised in Table 8.1. Typically, families are chosen who are rated high in EE and randomly assigned either to a family intervention, routine treatment, or a control treatment. The samples are then followed up for a period of at least 1 year and patients are monitored for episodes of relapse. In some of the studies patients' social functioning and quality of life has been assessed.

The results of these trials have been uniformly positive, with a reduction in the rate of relapse over 12 months from 60% down to between 25% and 33%. The results of these trials have been consistent and shown clinically highly significant improvements. Not only do these studies represent a major clinical advance but also provide striking support for the validity of the concept of EE as a predictor of relapse in people with schizophrenia.

TABLE 8.1

**Family intervention studies: Relapse rates for high EE households**

| Study | Relapse rates (%) | |
|---|---|---|
| | 9 or 12 months | 24 months |
| Camberwell study 1 | | |
| (Leff et al., 1982, 1985) | | |
| Family intervention | 8 | 20 |
| Routine treatment | 50 | 78 |
| Camberwell study 2 | | |
| (Leff et al., 1989, 1990) | | |
| Family therapy | 8 | 33 |
| Relatives groups | 17 | 36 |
| California-USC study | | |
| (Falloon et al., 1982, 1985) | | |
| Family intervention | 6 | 17 |
| Individual intervention | 44 | 83 |
| Pittsburgh study | | |
| (Hogarty et al., 1986) | | |
| Family intervention | 23 | (32) |
| Social skills training | 30 | (42) |
| Combined FI and SST | 9 | (25) |
| Control group | 41 | 66 |
| Salford study | | |
| (Tarrier et al., 1988, 1989) | | |
| Family intervention | 12(5) | 33(24) |
| Education programme | 43 | 57 |
| Routine treatment | 53 | 60 |
| China study | | |
| (Zhang et al., 1995) | 15 | |
| Family intervention | 54 | |

Percentages in parentheses represent "treatment takers" only, and exclude those who did not complete the intervention programme.

There has been much debate about the explanation for these impressive results. It has been pointed out, for example, that all the interventions involve not only changes to the family but also require the active participation of the patient. Relapse prevention strategies are a common feature and, in the trial of Falloon et al. (1982), it was noted that the patients receiving family intervention also demonstrated an improved compliance with medication regimes, which may have been partly responsible for the improved rate of relapse. However, as the research of Leff et al. (1989) demonstrates, the improvement in relapse is usually confined to those families where a reduction in expressed emotion has been achieved, suggesting that a significant part of the intervention is achieved through important changes in family relationships and psychosocial stress.

## Summary

- Helping people to cope with their symptoms reduces their severity and eases distress.
- It is possible to challenge and reality-test delusional beliefs provided this is done in a gentle and collaborative manner.
- Trials of cognitive-behavioural therapy using reality testing show a reduction in the strength of delusional beliefs.
- Relapse in psychosis is preceded by subtle changes in thinking and affect; these vary from person to person and are known as the "relapse signature".
- Early detection and intervention in relapse reduces the severity and probability of relapse.
- Family interventions in high EE homes reduce intrafamilial stress and subsequent psychotic relapse.

# Further reading

Birchwood, M., & Tarrier, N. (1994). *Psychological management of schizophrenia*. Chichester, UK: Wiley.

Birchwood, M., Fowler, D., & Jackson, C. (2000). *Early intervention in psychosis: A guide to concepts, evidence and interventions*. Chichester, UK: Wiley.

Chadwick, P., Birchwood, M., & Trower, P. (1996). *Cognitive therapy for delusions, voices and paranoia*. Chichester, UK: Wiley.

Fowler, D., Garety, P., & Kuipers, E. (1995). *Cognitive behaviour therapy for psychosis: Theory and practice*. Chichester, UK: Wiley.

Hirsh, S.R., & Weinberger, D.R. (1995). *Schizophrenia*. Oxford, UK: Blackwell Science.

Maj, M., & Sartorius, N. (1999). *Schizophrenia*. Chichester, UK: Wiley.

Mueser, K.T., & Tarrier, N. (1998). *Handbook of social functioning in schizophrenia*. Boston: Allyn & Bacon.

Warner, R. (1994). *Recovery from schizophrenia: Psychiatry and political economy*. New York: Routledge.

# References

Al-Issa, I. (1995). The illusion of reality or the reality of illusion: Hallucinations and culture. *British Journal of Psychiatry, 166*(3), 368–373.

Allebeck, P., Varla, A., & Wistedt, B. (1986). Suicide and violent death among patients with schizophrenia. *Acta Psychiatrica Scandinavica, 74*(1), 43–49.

Alvir, J.M., Woerner, M.G., Gudduz, H. et al. (1999). Obstetric complications predict treatment response in first-episode schizophrenia. *Psychological Medicine, 29*, 621–627.

American Psychiatric Association (1994). *Diagnostic and Statistical Manual of Mental Disorders* (4th ed.). Washington, DC: American Psychiatric Association.

Andreasen, N.C. (1982). Negative symptoms in schizophrenia: Definition and reliability. *Archives of General Psychiatry, 39*, 784–788.

Andreasen, N.C., Rezai, K., Alliger, R., Swayze, V.W., Flaum, M., Kirchner, P., Cohen, G., & O'Leary, D.S. (1992). Hypofrontality in neuroleptic-naïve patients and in-patients with chronic schizophrenia. *Archives of General Psychiatry, 49*, 943–958.

Angermeyer, M.C., Goldstein, J.M., & Kuhn, L. (1989). Gender differences in schizophrenia: Rehospitalisation and community survival. *Psychological Medicine, 19*, 365–382.

Angst, J., Scharfetter, C., & Stassen, H.H. (1983). Classification of schizo-affective patients by multidimensional scaling and cluster analysis. *Psychiatr. Clin. (Basel), 16*, 254–264.

Anthony, W.A., & Blanch, A. (1987). Supported employment for persons who are psychiatrically disabled: An historical and conceptual perspective. *Psychosocial Rehabilitation Journal, 11*, 5–23.

Arieti, S. (1955). *Interpretation of schizophrenia*. New York: Basic Books.

Asaad, G., & Shapiro, M.D. (1986). Hallucinations, theoretical and clinical overview. *American Journal of Psychiatry, 143*, 1088–1097.

Baker, C.A., & Morrison, A.P. (1998). Cognitive process in auditory hallucinations: Attributional biases and metacognition. *Psychological Medicine, 28*(5), 1199–1208.

Barnes, T.R.E., Curson, D.A., Liddle, P.R., & Patel, M. (1989). The nature and prevalence of depression in chronic schizophrenia in-patients. *British Journal of Psychiatry, 154*, 486–491.

Barnes, T.R.E., Milavic, G., Curson, D.A., & Plaff, S.D. (1983). Use of the Social Behaviour Assessment Schedule (SBAS) in a trial of maintenance antipsychotic therapy in schizophrenic outpatients: Pimozide versus fluphenazine. *Social Psychiatry, 18*, 193–199.

Barrowclough, C., & Tarrier, N. (1992). *Families of schizophrenic patients: Cognitive behavioural intervention*. London: Chapman & Hall.

Barrowclough, C., Tarrier, N., & Johnston,

M. (1996). Distress, expressed emotion, and attributions in relatives of schizophrenia patients. *Schizophrenia Bulletin, 22*(4), 691–702.

Bassuk, E.L., & Gerson, S. (1978). Deinstitutionalisation and mental health services. *Scientific American, 238,* 46–53.

Bateson, G., Jackson, D.D., Haley, J., & Weakland, J. (1956). Toward a history of schizophrenia. *Behavioural Science, 1,* 251–264.

Bebbington, P., & Kuipers, L. (1994). The predictive utility of expressed emotion in schizophrenia: An aggregate analysis. *Psychological Medicine, 24,* 707–718.

Bebbington, P., Wilkins, S., Jones P.B., Foerster, A., Murray, R.M., Toone, B., & Lewis, S. (1993). Life events and psychosis: Initial results from the Camberwell Collaborative Psychosis Study. *British Journal of Psychiatry, 162,* 72–79.

Beech, A., Baylis, G.C., Smithson, P., & Claridge, G. (1989). Individual differences in schizotypal on reflected in measures of cognitive inhibition. *British Journal of Clinical Psychology, 28.*

Beiser, M., Erickson, D., Fleming, J.A., & Iacono, W.G. (1993). Establishing the onset of psychotic illness. *American Journal of Psychiatry, 150,* 1349–1354.

Beiser, M., Fleming, J.A., Iacono, W.G., & Lin, T. (1988). Refining the diagnosis of schizophrenia form disorder. *American Journal of Psychiatry, 145,* 695–700.

Bentall, R.P. (1990). The syndromes and symptoms of psychosis: Or why you can't play "twenty questions" with the concept of schizophrenia and hope to win. In R.P. Bentall (Ed.), *Reconstructing schizophrenia.* London: Routledge.

Bentall, R.P., Claridge, G.S., & Slade, P.D. (1989). The multidimensional nature of schizotypal traits: A factor analytic study with normal subjects. *British*

*Journal of Clinical Psycholology, 28*(Pt. 4), 363–376.

Bentall, R.P., Jackson, F., & Pilgrim, D. (1988). Abandoning the concept of "schizophrenia": some implications of validity arguments for psychological research into psychotic phenomena. *British Journal of Clinical Psychology, 27,* 303–324.

Bentall, R.P., & Kaney, S. (1989). Content specific processing and persecutory delusions: An investigation using the emotional Stroop test. *British Journal of Medical Psychology, 62,* 355–364.

Bentall, R.P., Kaney, S., & Dewey, M.E. (1991). Persecutory delusions: An attribution theory analysis. *British Journal of Clinical Psychology, 30,* 13–23.

Bentall, R.P., & Slade, P.D. (1985). Reality testing and auditory hallucinations: A signal detection analysis. *British Journal of Clinical Psychology, 24,* 159–169.

Berman, K.F., Torrey, E.F., Daniel, D.G. et al. (1992). Regional cerebral blood-flow in monozygotic twins discordant and concordant for schizophrenia. *Archives of General Psychiatry, 49,* 927–934.

Birchwood, M.J. (1995). Early intervention in psychotic relapse: Cognitive approaches to detection and management. *Behaviour Change, 12,* 2–19.

Birchwood, M.J., & Chadwick, P.D. (1997). The omnipotence of voices: III. Testing the validity of the cognitive model. *Psychological Medicine, 27,* 1345–1353.

Birchwood, M.J., & Cochrane, R. (1990). Families coping with schizophrenia: Coping styles, their origins and correlates. *Psychological Medicine, 20,* 857–865.

Birchwood, M.J., Cochrane, R., MacMillan, J.F., Copestake, S., Kucharka, J., & Carris, M. (1992). The influence of ethnicity and family structure on relapse in first-episode schizophrenia: A comparison of Asian, Afro-

Caribbean, and white patients. *British Journal of Psychiatry, 161*, 783–790.

Birchwood, M.J., Fowler, D., & Jackson, C. (2000). *Early intervention in psychosis*. Chichester, UK: Wiley.

Birchwood, M.J., Hallett, S., & Preston, M. (1988). *Schizophrenia: An integrated approach to recommend treatment*. London: Longman.

Birchwood, M.J., & Iqbal, Z. (1998). Depression and suicidal thinking in psychosis: A cognitive approach. In T. Wykes, N. Tarrier, & S. Lewis (Eds), *Outcome and intervention in psychological treatment of schizophrenia*. Chichester, UK: Wiley.

Birchwood, M.J., Iqbal, Z., Chadwick, P., & Trower, P. (2000). Cognitive approach to depression and suicidal thinking in psychosis: I. Ontogeny of post-psychotic depression. *British Journal of Psychiatry, 177*, 516–528.

Birchwood, M.J., Mason, R., MacMillan, J.F., & Healy, J. (1993). Depression, demoralisation and control over psychotic illness: A comparison of deprived and non-deprived patients with a chronic psychosis. *Psychological Medicine, 23*, 387–395.

Birchwood, M.J., McGorry, P., & Jackson, H. (1997) Early intervention in schizophrenia. *British Journal of Psychiatry, 170*, 2–5.

Birchwood, M.J., & Preston, M. (1991). Schizophrenia. In W. Dryden, & R. Rentoul (Eds), *Adult clinical problems*. London: Routledge.

Birchwood, M.J., & Smith, J. (1987). Expressed emotion and first episodes of schizophrenia. *British Journal of Psychiatry, 151*, 859–860.

Birchwood, M.J., Smith, J., MacMillan, J.F. et al. (1989). Predicting relapse in schizophrenia: The development and implementation of an early signs monitoring system using patients and families as observers, a preliminary

investigation. *Psychological Medicine, 19*, 649–656.

Birchwood, M.J., & Spencer, E. (1999). Psychotherapies for schizophrenia: A review. In M. Maj, & N. Sartorius (Eds), *Schizophrenia*. Chichester, UK: Wiley.

Birley, J.L.T., & Brown, G.W. (1970). Crises and life changes preceding the onset of relapse of acute schizophrenia: Clinical aspects. *British Journal of Psychiatry, 116*, 327–333.

Bleuler, M. (1978). *The schizophrenic disorders, long-term patient and family studies*. [Die schizophrenia Geistess torvingen im lichte langjalriger Kranker—under familienge schichten]. (S.M. Clemens, Trans.). New Haven, CT: Yale University Press. (Original work published 1972)

Bogerts, B. (1989). The role of limbic and paralimbic pathology in the etiology of schizophrenia. *Psychology Research, 29*(3), 255–256.

Boklage, C.E. (1977). Schizophrenia, brain asymmetry development, and twinning: Cellular relationship with etiological and possibly prognostic implications. *Biological Psychiatry, 12*, 19–35.

Bond, G.R., Drake, R.E., Mueser, K.T., & Becker, D.R. (1997). An update on supported employment for people with severe mental illness: A review. *Psychiatric Services, 48*, 335–346.

Boyle, M. (1990). *Schizophrenia: A scientific delusion?* London: Routledge.

Breier, A., & Strauss, J.S. (1983). Self-control in psychotic disorders. *Archives of General Psychiatry, 40*, 1141–1145.

Breier, A., Schreiber, J.L., Dyer, J., & Pickar, D. (1991). National Institute of Mental Health longitudinal study of chronic schizophrenia: Prognosis and predictors of outcome. *Archives of General Psychiatry, 48*, 239–246.

Brockington, I.F., Roper, A., Copas, J., Buckley, M., Andrade, C.E., Wigg, P., Farmer, A., Kaufman, C., & Haawley, R.

(1991). Schizophrenia, bipolar disorder and depression: A discrimination analysis, using "lifetime" psychopathology ratings. *British Journal of Psychiatry, 159,* 485–494.

Brown, G.W. (1959). Experiences of discharged chronic schizophrenic mental hospital patients in various types of living group. *Millbank Memorial Quarterly, 37,* 105–131.

Brown, G., & Birbey, J. (1968). Crises and life changes and the onset of schizophrenia. *Journal of Health and Social Behaviour, 9,* 203–214.

Brown, G.W., Birley, J.L.T., & Wing, J.K. (1972). The influence of family life on the course of schizophrenic disorders: A replication. *British Journal of Psychiatry, 121,* 241–258.

Brown, G.W., Bone, M., Dalison, B., & Wing, J.K. (1966). *Schizophrenia and social care* (Maudsley Monographs, No. 17). London: Oxford University Press.

Brown, G.W., Carstairs, G.M., & Topping, G.C. (1958). The post hospital adjustment of chronic mental patients. *Lancet, ii,* 685–689.

Brown, G.W., & Harris, T.O. (1978). *Social origins of depression.* London: Tavistock.

Brown, G.W., Monck, E.M., Carstairs, G.M., & Wing, J.K. (1962). The influence of family life on the course of schizophrenic illness. *British Journal of Preventative and Social Medicine, 16,* 55–68.

Campbell, J.D. (1953). *Manic-depressive defeat: Clinical and psychiatric significance.* Philadelphia: J.B. Lippincott.

Carpenter, W.T., Hanlon, T., Heinrichs, D.W., Kirkpatrick, B., Levine, J., & Buchanan, R. (1990). Continuous versus targeted medication in schizophrenic patients: Outcome results. *American Journal of Psychiatry, 147,* 1138–1148.

Carpenter, W.T., Heinrichs, D.W., & Wayman, A. (1988). Deficit and non deficit forms of schizophrenia: The concept. *American Journal of Psychiatry, 145,* 578–583.

Carpenter, W.T., & Strauss, J.S. (1991). The prediction of outcome in schizophrenia: IV. Eleven-year follow-up of the Washington IPSS cohort. *Journal of Nervous and Mental Disease, 179,* 517–525.

Castle, D.J., & Murray, R.M. (1991). The neurodevelopmental basis of sex differences in schizophrenia. *Psychological Medicine, 21,* 565–575.

Castle, D.J., Scott, K., Wessely, S., & Murray, R.M. (1993). Does social deprivation during gestation and early life predispose to later schizophrenia? *Social Psychiatry and Psychiatric Epidemiology, 28,* 1–4.

Castle, D.J., Wessely, S., Van Os, J., & Murray, R.M. (1998). *Psychosis in the inner city: The Camberwell First Episode study* (Maudsley Monographs, No. 40). Hove, UK: Psychology Press.

Chadwick, P., & Birchwood, M.J. (1994). The omnipotence of voices: A cognitive approach to auditory hallucinations. *British Journal of Psychiatry, 164,* 190–201.

Chadwick, P., Birchwood, M., & Trower, P. (1996). *Cognitive therapy for delusions, voices and paranoia,* Chichester, UK: John Wiley and Sons.

Chadwick, P.D.J., & Lowe, C.F. (1990). Measurement and modification of delusional beliefs. *Journal of Consulting and Clinical Psychology, 58,* 225–232.

Chakos, M.H., Mayerhoff, D.I., Loebel, A.D., Alvir, J.M., & Lieberman, J.A. (1993). Incidence and correlates of acute extrapyramidal symptoms in first episode of schizophrenia. *Psychopharmacology Bulletin, 28,* 81–86.

Champion, A., & Power, M.J. (1995). Social and cognitive approaches to depression. Towards a new synthesis. *British Journal of Clinical Psychology, 34,* 485–503.

Chapman, L.J., & Chapman, J.P. (1985).

Psychosis proneness. In M. Alpert (Ed.), *Controversies in schizophrenia*. New York: Guilford Press.

Chintalapudi, M., Kulhara, P., & Avestri, A. (1993). Post-psychotic depression in schizophrenia. *European Archives of Psychiatry and Clinical Neuroscience, 243*, 103–108.

Chittick, R.A., Brooks, G.W., Irons, F.S., & Deane, W.N. (1961). *The Vermont story*. Burlington, VT: Queen City Printers.

Chung, R.K., Langeluddecke, P., & Tennant, C. (1986). Threatening life events in the onset of schizophreniform psychosis and hypomania. *British Journal of Psychiatry, 148*, 680–686.

Ciompi, L. (1980). The natural history of schizophrenia in the long-term. *British Journal of Psychiatry, 136*, 413–420.

Ciompi, L., & Müller, C. (1984). *The life and course and aging in schizophrenia: A catamnestic longitudinal study into advanced age* [Lebensweg under alter schizophrenia. Eine katamnestische bis ins alter]. (E. Forberg, Trans.). Vermont Longitudinal Research Project. (Original work published 1976)

Claridge, G. (1990). Can a disease model of schizophrenia survive? In R.P. Bentall (Ed.), *Reconstructing schizophrenia*. London: Routledge.

Claridge, G. (1997). *Schizotypy: Implications for illness and health*. Oxford: Oxford University Press.

Clarke, A.M., & Clarke, A.D.B. (1974). Genetic–environmental interactions in cognitive development. In A.M. Clarke, & A.D.B. Clarke (Eds), *Mental deficiency: The changing outlook*. London: Methuen.

Cloninger, C.R. (1994). Turning point in the design of linkage studies of schizophrenia. *American Journal of Medical Genetics, 54*, 83–92.

Close, H., & Garety, P.A. (1998). Cognitive assessment of voices: Further developments in understanding the emotional impact of voices. *British Journal of Clinical Psychology, 37*, 173–188.

Cochrane, R. (1983). *The social creation of mental illness*. Harlow, UK: Longman.

Cochrane, R., & Singh Bal, S. (1987). Migration and schizophrenia: An examination of five hypotheses. *Social Psychiatry, 22*, 181–191.

Cole, E., Leavey, G., King, M., Johnson-Sabine, E., & Hoar, A. (1995). Pathways to care for patients with a first episode of psychosis: A comparison of ethnic groups. *British Journal of Psychiatry, 167*, 770–776.

Corrigan, P.W., & Green, M.F. (1993). Schizophrenic patients' sensitivity to social clues: The role of abstraction. *American Journal of Psychiatry, 150*, 589–594.

Costello, C.G. (1992). *Symptoms of schizophrenia*. New York: John Wiley & Sons.

Craig, T. (1998). Models of case management and their impact on social outcomes of severe mental illness. In K.T. Mueser, & N. Tarrier (Eds), *Handbook of social functioning in schizophrenia*. Boston: Allyn & Bacon.

Cross, A.J., Crow, T.J., Killpack, W.S., Longden, A., Owen, F., & Riley, G.J. (1978). The activities of brain dopamine $\beta$-hydroxylase and catechol-o-methyltransferase in schizophrenia and controls. *Psychopharmacology, 59*, 117–121.

Crow, T.J. (1980). Molecular pathology of schizophrenia: More than one disease process? *British Medical Journal, 280*, 66–68.

Crow, T.J. (1986). The continuum of psychosis and its implications for the structure of the gene. *British Journal of Psychiatry, 149*, 419–429.

Crow, T.J. (1990). The continuum of psychosis and its genetic origins: The sixty-fifth Maudsley Lecture. *British Journal of Psychiatry, 156*, 788–797.

Crow, T.J., MacMillan, J.F., Johnson, A.L.,

& Johnstone, E.C. (1986). The Northwick Park study of first episodes of schizophrenia: I. A randomised controlled trial of prophylactic neuroleptic treatment. *British Journal of Psychiatry, 148*, 120–127.

Cutting, J., & Charlish, A. (1995). *Schizophrenia: Understanding and coping with the illness*. London: Thortons.

Davidson, L., Stayner, D., & Haglund, K.E. (1998). Phenomological perspectives on the social functioning of people with schizophrenia. In K.T. Mueser, & N. Tarrier (Eds), *Handbook of social functioning in schizophrenia*. Boston: Allyn & Bacon.

Davis, J.M., & Garver, D.L. (1978). Neuroleptics: Clinical use in psychiatry. In L. Iversen, S. Iversen, & S. Snyder (Eds), *Handbook of psychopharmacology*. New York: Plenum Press.

Day, R. (1989). Schizophrenia. In G.W. Brown, & T.O. Harris (Eds), *Life events and illness* (pp. 113–137). London: Unwin Hyman.

Day, R., Neilsen, J.A., & Korten, A. (1987). Stressful life events preceding the acute onset of schizophrenia: A cross national study from the World Health Organization. *Culture, Medicine and Psychiatry, 11*, 123–206.

Deakin, J.F.W., Slater, P., Simpson, M.D.C., Gilchrist, A.C., Skan, W.J., Royston, M.C., Reynolds, G.P., & Cross, A.J. (1989). Frontal cortical and left temporal glutamatergic dysfunction in schizophrenia. *Journal of Neurochemistry, 52*, 1781–1786.

Deakin, J.F.W., Slater, P., Simpson, M.D.C., & Royston, M.C. (1990). Disturbed brain glutamate and GABA mechanisms in schizophrenia. *Schizophrenia Research, 3*(1), 33.

DeSisto, M.J., Harding, C.M., McCormick, R.V., Ashikaga, T., & Brooks, G.W. (1995). The Maine and Vermont three-decade studies of serious mental illness: I. Matched comparison of cross-sectional outcome. *British Journal of Psychiatry, 167*, 331–338.

Done, D.J., Johnstone, E.C., Frith, C.D., Golding, J., Shepherd, P.M., & Crow, T.J. (1991). Complications of pregnancy and delivery in relation to psychosis in adult life: Data from the British perinatal mortality survey sample. *British Medical Journal, 302*, 1576–1580.

Donohoe, C.P., Carter, M.J., Bloem, W.D., & Wallace, C.J. (1991). Assessment of interpersonal problem-solving skills. *Psychiatry, 53*, 329–339.

Drake, R.E., Brunette, M.F., & Mueser, K.T. (1998). Substance use disorders and social functioning in schizophrenia. In K.T. Mueser, & N. Tarrier (Eds), *Handbook of social function in schizophrenia*. Boston: Allyn & Bacon.

Drake, R., Haddock, G.R., Hopkins, R., & Lewis, S. (1998). The measurement of outcome in schizophrenia. In T. Wykes, N. Tarrier, & S. Lewis (Eds), *Outcome and innovation in psychological treatment of schizophrenia*. Chichester, UK: Wiley.

Drury, V., Birchwood, M.J., Cochrane, R. et al. (1996). Cognitive therapy and recovery from acute psychosis: A controlled trial. II. Impact on recovery time. *British Journal of Psychiatry, 169*, 602–607.

Edgerton, R.B., & Cohen, A. (1994). Culture and schizophrenia – the DOSMD challenge. *British Journal of Psychiatry, 164*, 222–231.

Eisenberg, M.G., & Cole, H.W. (1986). A behavioural approach to job seeking for psychiatrically impaired persons. *Journal of Rehabilitation, 27*, 46–49.

Erickson, D.H., Beiser, M., Iacono, W.G., Fleming, J.A.E., & Lin, T. (1989). The role of social relationships in the course of first episode schizophrenia and affective psychosis. *American Journal of Psychiatry, 146*, 1456–1461.

Erlenmeyer-Kimling, L. (1987). High-risk research in schizophrenia: A summary of what has been learned. *Journal of Psychiatric Research, 21*, 401–411.

Fadden, G. (1998). Family intervention in psychosis. *Journal of Mental Health, 7*(2), 115–122.

Falkai, P., & Bogerts, B. (1992). Neurodevelopmental abnormalities in schizophrenia. *Clinical Neuropharmacology, 15* (Suppl. 1, Pt. A), 498A–499A.

Falloon, I.R., Boyd, J.L., McGill, C.W. et al. (1982). Family management in the prevention of exacerbations of schizophrenia – a controlled study. *New England Journal of Medicine, 306*, 1437–1440.

Falloon, I.R., Boyd, J.L., McGill, C.W., Williamson, M., Razani, J., Moss, H.B., Gilderman, A.M., & Simpson, G.M. (1985). Family management in the prevention of morbidity of schizophrenia: Clinical outcome of a two-year longitudinal study. *Archives of General Psychiatry, 42*, 887–896.

Falloon, I.R., & Pedersen, J. (1985). Family management in the prevention of morbidity of schizophrenia: The adjustment of the family unit. *British Journal of Psychiatry, 147*, 156–163.

Falloon, I.R., & Talbot, R.E. (1981). Persistent auditory hallucinations – coping mechanisms and implications for management. *Psychological Medicine, 11*, 329–339.

Farmer, A.E., McGuffin, P., & Gottesman, I.I. (1987). Twin concordance for DSM-III schizophrenia: Scrutinising the validity of the definition. *Archives of General Psychiatry, 44*, 634–641.

Fennig, S., Kovasznay, B., Rich, C., Ram, R., Pato, C., Miller, A., Rubinstein, J., Carlson, G.A., Schwartz, J., Phelan, J., Lavelle, J., Craig, T.K.J., & Bromet, E.J. (1995). Six months stability of psychiatric diagnosis in first admission patients with psychosis. *American Journal of Psychiatry, 151*, 1200–1208.

Fenton, F.R., Tessier, L., Struening, E.L., Smith, F.A., & Benoit, C. (1982). *Home and Hospital Psychiatric Treatment,* London: Croom Helm.

Fenton, W.S., & McGlashen, T.H. (1987). Proquestic scale for chronic schizophrenia. *Schizophrenia Bulletin, 13*, 277–286.

Fish, B., Marcus, J., Hans, S.L., Auerbach, J.G., & Perdue, S. (1992). Infants at risk for schizophrenia: Sequel of a genetic neurointegrative defect. A review and replication analysis of pandysmaturation in the Jerusalem infant development study. *Archives of General Psychiatry, 49*, 221–235.

Flor-Henry, P. (1983). Determinants of psychosis in epilepsy: Laterality and forced normalisation. *Biological Psychiatry, 18*, 1045–1057.

Foucault, M. (1965). *Madness and civilisation.* New York: Pantheon.

Foulds, G.A., & Bedford, A. (1975). Hierarchy of classes of personal illness. *Psychological Medicine, 5*, 181–192.

Fowler, D.G., Garety, P., & Kuipers, E. (1995). *Cognitive behaviour therapy for psychosis: Theory and practice.* Chichester, UK: John Wiley and Sons.

Freeman, H. (1978). Pharmacological treatment and management. In J.K. Wing (Ed.), *Schizophrenia: Towards a new synthesis.* London: Academic Press.

Frith, C.D. (1987). The positive and negative symptoms of schizophrenia reflect impairments in the perception and initiation of action. *Psychological Medicine, 17*, 631–648.

Frith, C.D. (1992). *The cognitive neuropsychology of schizophrenia.* Hove, UK: Lawrence Erlbaum Associates Ltd.

Fromm-Reichman, F. (1948). Notes on the development of treatment of schizophrenia by psychoanalytic psychotherapy. *Psychiatry, 11*, 263–273.

Gaebel, W. (1995). Is intermittent, early intervention medication an alternative for neuroleptic maintenance treatment?

*International Clinical Psychopharmacology, 9*(Suppl. 5), 11–16.

Gaebel, W., Frick, U., Kopoke, W. et al. (1993). Early neuroleptic intervention in schizophrenia – are prodromal symptoms valid predictors of relapse? *British Journal of Psychiatry, 163*, 8–12.

Garety, P.A. (1991). Reasoning and delusions. *British Journal of Psychiatry, 159*(Suppl.), 14–18.

Garety, P.A., & Freeman, D. (1999). Cognitive approaches to delusions: A critical review of theories and evidence. *British Journal of Clinical Psychology, 38*, 113–154.

Gelder, M., Gath, D., & Mayou, R. (1989). Paranoid symptoms and paranoid syndromes. In M. Gelder, D. Gath, & R. Mayou (Eds), *Oxford textbook of psychiatry* (2nd edn, pp. 324–344). Oxford: Oxford University Press.

Gershon, E.S., De Lisi, L.E., Hamovit, J., Nurnberger, J.L., Maxwell, M.E., & Schreiber, J. (1988). A controlled study of chronic psychoses: Schizophrenia and schizoaffective disorder. *Archives of General Psychiatry, 45*, 328–336.

Gillin, J.C., Kaplan, J.A., & Wyatt, R.J. (1976). Clinical effects of tryptophan in chronic schizophrenia. *Biological Psychiatry, 11*, 635–639.

Glasscote, R.M., Cumming, E., & Rutman, I. (1979). *Sheltered workshop study: Vol. II. Study of handicapped clients in sheltered workshops and recommendations of the secretary*. Washington, DC: American Psychiatric Association.

Glynn, S.M., & MacKain, S. (1992). Training life skills. In D. Kavanagh (Ed.), *Schizophrenia: An overview and practical handbook*. London: Chapman & Hall.

Goldsmith, J.B., & McFool, R.M. (1975). Development and evaluation of an interpersonal skill-training programme for psychiatric inpatients. *Journal of Abnormal Psychology, 84*, 51–58.

Goldstein, J.M. (1992). Gender and schizophrenia: A summary of findings. *Schizophrenia Monitor, 2*(2).

Goldstein, J.M., Faraone, S.V., Chen, W.J., & Tsuang, M.T. (1992). Gender and the familial risk for schizophrenia: Disentangling confounding factors. *Schizophrenia Research, 7*, 135–140.

Goodwin, F.K., & Jamison, K. (1992). *Manic-depressive illness*. Oxford: Oxford University Press.

Gottesman, I.I., & Shields, J. (1972). *Schizophrenia and genetics: A twin vantage point*. New York: Academic Press.

Gottesman, I.I., & Shields, J. (1982). *Schizophrenia: The epi-genetic puzzle*. Cambridge: Cambridge University Press.

Grad, J., & Sainsbury, P. (1968). The effects that patients have on their families in a community care and a control psychiatric service: A two year follow up. *British Journal of Psychiatry, 114*, 265–278.

Gray, J.A. (1982). *The neuropsychology of anxiety: An enquiry into the functions of the septo-hippocampal system*. Oxford: Oxford University Press.

Gray, J.A., Feldon, L., Rawlins, J.N.P., Hemsley, D.R., & Smith, A.D. (1990). The neuropsychology of schizophrenia. *Behavioural and Brain Sciences, 14*, 1–84.

Haas, G.L., & Garratt, L.S. (1998). Gender differences in social functioning. In K.T. Mueser, & N. Tarrier (Eds), *Handbook of social functioning in schizophrenia*. Boston: Allyn & Bacon.

Hagen, D.Q. (1983). The relationship between job loss and physical and mental illness. *Hosp. Community Psychiatry, 34*(5), 438–441.

Halford, W.K., & Hayes, R.L. (1992). Social skills training with schizophrenic patients. In D.J. Kavanagh (Ed.), *Schizophrenia: An overview and practical handbook*. London: Chapman & Hall.

Hambrecht, M., Maurer, K., Hafner, H., & Sartorius, N. (1992). Transnational stability of gender differences in schizophrenia? An analysis based on the WHO study of determinants of outcome of severe mental disorders. *European Archives of Psychological Clinical Neuroscience, 242*, 6–12.

Hammeke, T.A., McQuillen, M.P., & Cohen, B.A. (1983). Musical hallucinations association with acquired deafness. *Journal of Neurology, Neurosurgery and Psychiatry, 46*, 570–572.

Hammen, C. (1997). *Depression*. Hove, UK: Psychology Press.

Hardesty, J., Falloon, I.R.H., & Shirin, K. (1985). The impact of life events, stress and coping on the morbidity of schizophrenia. In I.R. Falloon (Ed.), *Family management of schizophrenia*. Baltimore: Johns Hopkins University Press.

Harding, C.M., & Keller, A.B. (1998). Long term outcome of social functioning. In K.T. Mueser, & N. Tarrier (Eds), *Handbook of social functioning in schizophrenia*. Needham Heights, MA: Allyn & Bacon.

Harding, C.M., Brooks, G.W., Ashikaga, T., Strauss, J.S., & Breier, A. (1987). The Vermont longitudinal study of persons with severe mental illness: Methodology, study sample and overall status 32 years later. *American Journal of Psychiatry, 144*, 718–726.

Harris, D., & Batki, S.L. (2000). Stimulant psychosis: Symptom profile and acute clinical course. *American Journal on Addictions, 9*, 28–37.

Harrison, G., Croudace, T., Mason, P., Blazebrook, C., & Medley, I. (1996). Predicting the long-term outcome of schizophrenia. *Psychological Medicine, 26*, 697–705.

Hatfield, A.B. (1978). Psychological costs of schizophrenia to the family. *Social Work, 23*, 355–359.

Hawks, D. (1975). Community care: An analysis of assumptions. *British Journal of Psychiatry, 127*, 276–285.

Heckers, S., Heinsen, H., Heinsen, Y., & Beckman, H. (1991). Cortex white matter, and base ganglia in schizophrenia: A volumetric post mortem study. *Biological Psychiatry, 29*, 556–566.

Hegarty, J.D., Baldessarini, R.J., Tohen, M., Waternaux, C., & Oepen, G. (1994). One hundred years of schizophrenia: A meta-analysis of the outcome literature. *American Journal of Psychiatry, 151*, 1409–1416.

Heinrichs, D.W., & Carpenter, W.T., Jr. (1985). Prospective study of prodromal symptoms in schizophrenic relapse. *American Journal of Psychiatry, 142*, 371–373.

Hemsley, D. (1993a). Perceptual and cognitive abnormalities as the basis for schizophrenic symptoms. In A.S. David, & J. Cutting (Eds), *The neuropsychology of schizophrenia*. Hove, UK: Lawrence Erlbaum Associates Ltd.

Hemsley, D. (1993b). Schizophrenia: Interventions. In S.J.E. Lindsay, & G.E. Powell (Eds), *A handbook of clinical adult psychology*. London: Routledge.

Hemsley, D. (1994). A cognitive model for schizophrenia and its possible neural basis. *Acta Psychiatrica Scandinavica* (Suppl. 384), 80–86.

Henderson, S., Byrne, D.G., & Duncan-Jones, P. (1981). *Neurosis and the social environment*. Toronto: Academic Press.

Herson, M., & Bellack, A.S. (1976). Social skills training for chronic psychiatric patients: Rationale, research findings and future directions. *Comprehensive Psychiatry, 17*, 559–580.

Herz, M.I., & Melville, C. (1980). Relapse in schizophrenia. *American Journal of Psychiatry, 137*, 801–805.

Heston, L.L. (1966). Psychiatric disorders in foster home reared children of schizophrenic mothers. *British Journal of Psychiatry, 122*, 819–825.

Higgins, E.T. (1987). Self-discrepancy: A

theory relating self and affect. *Psychological Review, 94*, 319–340.

Hirsch, S., Bowen, J., Emami, J. et al. (1996). A one year prospective study of the effect of life events and medication in the aetiology of schizophrenic relapse. *British Journal of Psychiatry, 168*, 49–56.

Hirsch, S.R., & Weinberger, D.R. (1995). *Schizophrenia*. Oxford: Blackwell Science Ltd.

Hogarty, G.E., Anderson, C.M., Reiss, D.J., Kornblith, S.J., Greenwald, D.P., Javna, C.D., & Madonia, M.J. (1986). Family psychoeducation, social skills training, and maintenance chemotherapy in the aftercare treatment of schizophrenia, I: One-year effects of a controlled study on relapse and expressed emotion. *Archives of General Psychiatry, 43*, 633–642.

Hogarty, G.E., Anderson, C., Reiss, D., Kornblith, S., Greenwald, D., Ulrich, R., & Carter, M. (1991). Family psychoeducation, social skills training and maintenance chemotherapy in the aftercare treatment of schizophrenia: II. Two-year effects of a controlled study on relapse and adjustment. *Archives of General Psychiatry, 48*, 340–347.

Hogarty, G.E., Goldberg, S.C., & Schooler, N.R. (1974). Drug and sociotherapy in the aftercare of schizophrenic patients: III. Adjustment of non relapsed patients. *Archives of General Psychiatry, 31*, 609–618.

Hogarty, G.E., & Ulrich, R.F. (1977). Temporal effects of drug and placebo in delaying relapse in schizophrenic outpatients. *Archives of General Psychiatry, 34*, 297–301.

Hollis, C. (1995). Child and adolescent (juvenile onset) schizophrenia: A case control study of premorbid developmental impairments. *British Journal of Psychiatry, 166*, 489–495.

Holmes, T.H., & Rahe, R.H. (1967). The social readjustment rating scale. *Journal of Psychosomatic Research, 11*, 213–218.

Hoult, J., & Reynolds, I. (1983). *Psychiatric hospital vs community treatment: A controlled study*. NSW, Australia: Department of Health.

Huber, G., Gross, G., & Schuttler, R. (1975). A long-term follow-up study of schizophrenia: Psychiatric course of illness and prognosis. *Acta Psychiatrica Scandinavica, 50*, 49–57.

Huq, S.F., Garety, P.A., & Hemsley, D.R. (1988). Probabilistic judgements in deluded and non-deluded subjects. *Quarterly Journal of Experimental Psychology, 40A*, 801–812.

Hyde, L., Bridges, K., Goldberg, D., Lowson, K., Sterling, L., & Farragher, B. (1987). The evaluation of a hostel ward: A controlled study using modified cost-benefit analysis. *British Journal of Psychiatry, 151*, 805–12.

Iacono, W.G., & Beiser, M. (1992). Are males more likely than females to develop schizophrenia? *Journal of Psychiatry, 149*(8), 1070–1074.

Ingraham, L.J., Kugelmass, S., Frenkel, E., Nathan, M., & Mirsky, A.F. (1995). Twenty-five-year follow up of the Israeli high-risk study: Current and lifetime psychopathology. *Schizophrenia Bulletin, 21*, 183–192.

Jablensky, A. (1995). Schizophrenia: The epidemiological horizon. In S.R. Hirsch, & D.R. Weinberger (Eds), *Schizophrenia*. Oxford: Blackwell Science.

Jablensky, A., Sartorius, N., Ernberg, G. et al. (1992). Schizophrenia manifestations, incidence and course in different cultures. A World Health Organisation ten-country study. *Psycholological Medicine* (Monograph suppl.).

Jackson, C.P., & Birchwood, M.J. (1996). Early intervention in psychosis: Opportunities for secondary prevention. *British Journal of Clinical Psychology, 35*, 487–502.

Jackson, C.P., & Farmer, A. (1998). Early intervention in psychosis. *Journal of Mental Health, 7*, 157–164.

Jackson, C.P., & Iqbal, Z. (2000). Psychological and adjustment to early psychosis. In M. Birchwood, D. Fowler, & C. Jackson (Eds), *Early intervention in psychosis*. Chichester, UK: Wiley.

Jacobs, H.E., Liberman, R.P., Arruda, M.J., & Mintz, J. (1990). *The Job Finding Club: Predictors of outcome*. Presented to the 143rd Annual Meeting of the American Psychiatric Association, New York.

Jacobs, S., & Myers, J. (1976). Recent life events and acute schizophrenic psychosis: A controlled study. *Journal of Nervous and Mental Disease, 162*, 75–87.

Jernigan, T.L., Zisook, S., Heaton, R.K., Moranville, J.T., Hesselink, J.R., & Braff, D.L. (1991). Magnetic resonance imaging abnormalities in lenticular nuclei and cerebral cortex in schizophrenia. *Archives of General Psychiatry, 48*, 881–890.

Johnson, D. (1981). Studies of depressive symptoms in schizophrenia. *British Journal of Psychiatry, 139*, 89–101.

Johnson, D.A.W., Ludlow, J.M., Street, K., et al. (1987) Double-blind comparison of half-dose and standard-dose Fluphenixol Decanoate in the maintenance treatment of stabilised out-patients with schizophrenia. *British Journal of Psychiatry, 151*, 634–638.

Johnstone, E.C. (1991). What is crucial for the long-term outcome of schizophrenia? In H. Hüfner, & W.F. Gattaz (Eds), *Search for the causes of schizophrenia* (Vol. 2, pp. 67–76). Berlin: Springer.

Johnstone, E.C., Crow, T.J., Frith, C.D., Husband, J., & Kreel, L. (1976). Cerebral ventricular size and cognitive impairment in chronic schizophrenia. *Lancet, 2*, 924–926.

Johnstone, E.C., Crow, T.J., Frith, C.D., Carney, M.W., & Price, J.S. (1978). Mechanism of the antipsychotic effect in the treatment of acute schizophrenia. *Lancet*, 848–851.

Johnstone, E.C., Crow, T.J., Johnson, A.L., & MacMillan, J.F. (1986). The Northwick Park study of first episode schizophrenia: I. Presentation of the illness and problems relating to admission. *British Journal of Psychiatry, 148*, 115–120.

Jolley, A.G., Hirsch, S.R., Morrison, E. et al. (1990). Trial of brief intermittent neuroleptic prophylaxis for selected schizophrenic outpatients: Clinical and social outcome at two years. *British Medical Journal, 301*, 837–842.

Jones, P., Rodgers, B., Murray, R.M., & Marmot, M. (1994). Child development risk factors for adult schizophrenia in the British 1946 birth cohort. *Lancet, 344*, 1398–1402.

Kallman, F.J. (1938). *The genetics of schizophrenia*. New York: Augustin.

Kane, J.M. (1987). Treatment of schizophrenia. *Schizophrenia Bulletin, 13*, 133–156.

Kane, J.M. (1999). Olanzapine in the long-term treatment of schizophrenia. *British Journal of Psychiatry* (Supplement, 1999), *37*, 26–29.

Kane, J.M., Rifkin, A., & Woerner, M. (1983). Low dose neuroleptic treatment of outpatient schizophrenia. *Archives of General Psychiatry, 40*, 893–896.

Kaney, S., Wolfenden, M., Dewey, M.E., & Bentall, R.P. (1992). Persecutory delusions and the recall of threatening and non-threatening propositions. *British Journal of Clinical Psychology, 31*, 85–87.

Karno, M., & Jenkins, J.H. (1983). Cross-cultural issues in the course and treatment of schizophrenia. *Psychiatric Clinics of North America, 16*, 339–350.

Karno, M., Jenkins, J.H., de la Selva, A., Santana, F., Telles, C., Lopez, S., & Mintz, J. (1987). Expressed emotion and schizophrenic outcome among Mexican-American families. *Journal of*

*Nervous and Mental Disease*, 175, 143–151.

Kavanagh, D.J. (1992). *Schizophrenia: An overview and practical handbook*. London: Chapman & Hall.

Kendell, R. (1975). *The role of diagnosis in psychiatry*. London: Blackwell.

Kendell, R.E., & Brockington, I.F. (1980). The identification of disease entities and the relationship between schizophrenic and affective psychoses. *British Journal of Psychiatry*, 137, 324–331.

Kendell, R.E., Brockington, I.F., & Leff, J.P. (1979). Prognostic implications of six alternative definitions of schizophrenia. *Archives of General Psychiatry*, 36, 25–31.

Kendell, R.E., & Gourlay, J.A. (1970). The clinical distinction between the affective psychoses and schizophrenia. *British Journal of Psychiatry*, 117, 261–266.

Kendler, K.S., & Gruenberg, A.M. (1984). An independent antigen of the Danish adoption study of schizophrenia, VI. *Archives of General Psychiatry*, 41, 555–564.

Keshavan, M.S., Montrose, D.M., Pierri, J.N., Dick, K.L., Rosenberg, B., & Talagala, L. (1997). Magnetic resonance imaging and spectroscopy in offspring at risk for schizophrenia: Preliminary studies. *Progress in Neuro-Psychopharmacology & Biological Psychiatry*, 21, 1285–1295.

Kety, S.S., Rosenthal, D., Wender, P.H., Schulsinger, F., & Jacobsen, B. (1975). Mental illness in the biological and adoptive families of adopted individuals who have psychiatric interviews. In R.R. Fiene, D. Rosenthal, & H. Brill (Eds), *Genetic research in psychiatry* (pp. 147–165). Baltimore: Johns Hopkins University Press.

Kety, S.S., Rosenthal, D., Wender, P.H., Schulsinger, F., & Jacobsen, B. (1976). Mental illness in the biological and adoptive families of individuals who

have become schizophrenic. *Behaviour Genetics*, 6, 219–225.

Kinderman, P. (1994). Attentional bias, persecutory delusions and the self-concept. *British Journal of Medical Psychology*, 67, 53–66.

Kinderman, P., & Bentall, R.P. (1996). A new measure of causal locus: The internal, personal and situational attributions questionnaire. *Personality and Individual Differences*, 20, 261–264.

Kindness, K., & Newton, A. (1984). Patients and social skills groups: Is social skills training enough? *Behavioural Psychotherapy*, 12, 212–222.

Kingdon, D.G., & Turkington, D. (1994). *Cognitive-behavioral therapy of schizophrenia*. Hove, UK: Psychology Press.

Kleinman, A. (1987). Anthropology and psychiatry: The role of culture in cross-cultural research on illness. *British Journal of Psychiatry*, 151, 447–454.

Kuipers, L., & Bebbington, P.E. (1994). Expressed emotion research in Theoretical and clinical implications. *Psychological Medicine*, 18(4), 893–909.

Kuipers, E., Garety, P., Fowler, D. et al. (1997). London East Anglia randomised controlled trial of cognitive-behavioural therapy fo psychosis – 1. Effects of the treatment phase. *British Journal of Psychiatry*, 171, 319–327.

Kulhara, P., & Wig, N.N. (1978). The chronicity of schizophrenia in Northwest India: Results of a follow-up study. *British Journal of Psychiatry*, 132, 186–190.

Laing, R.D. (1967). *The politics of experience*. Harmondsworth, UK: Penguin.

Laruelle, M., Abi-Dargham, A., Gasanova, M., Toti, R., Weinberger, D.R., & Kleinman, J.E. (1993). Selective abnormality of prefrontal serotonergic receptors in schizophrenia: A post mortem study. *Archives of General Psychiatry*, 50, 810–818.

Lavender, A., & Holloway, F. (1992).

Models of continuing care. In M. Birchwood, & N. Tarrier (Eds), *Innovations in the psychological management of schizophrenia: Assessment, treatment and services*. Chichester, UK: Wiley.

Leff, J. (1982). *Psychiatry around the globe: A transcultural view*. New York: Marcel Dekker.

Leff, J., Berkowitz, R., Shavit, N., Strachan, A., Glass, I., & Vaughn, C. (1989). A trial of family therapy v a relatives group for schizophrenia. *British Journal of Psychiatry*, 154, 58–66.

Leff, J., Dayson, D., Gooch, C., Thornicroft, G., & Wills, W. (1996). Quality of life of long-stay patients discharged from two psychiatric institutions. *Psychiatric Services*, 47(1), 62–67.

Leff, J., Hirsch, S.R., Gaind, R., Rohde, P.D., & Stevens, B.C. (1973). Life events and maintenance therapy in schizophrenic relapse. *British Journal of Psychiatry*, 123, 659–660.

Leff, J., Kuipers, L., Berkowitz, R., Eberlein-Vries, R., & Sturgeon, D. (1982). A controlled trial of social intervention in the families of schizophrenic patients. *British Journal of Psychiatry*, 141, 121–134.

Leff, J., Kuipers, L., Berkowitz, R., & Sturgeon, D. (1985). A controlled trial of social intervention in the families of schizophrenic patients: Two year follow-up. *British Journal of Psychiatry*, 146, 594–600.

Leff, J., & Vaughn, C.E. (1980). The interaction of life events and relatives' expressed emotion in schizophrenia and depressive neurosis. *British Journal of Psychiatry*, 136, 146–153.

Leff, J., Wig, N.N., Ghosh, A. et al. (1990). III. Influence of relatives expressed emotion on the course of schizophrenia in Chandigarh. *British Journal of Psychiatry*, 156, 166–173.

Leff, J., & Wing, J.K. (1971). Trial of maintenance therapy in schizophrenia. *British Medical Journal*, 3, 599–604.

Lewis, S.W. (1990). Computed tomography in schizophrenia fifteen years on. *British Journal of Psychiatry*, 157(Suppl. 9), 16–24.

Lewis, S.W., & Murray, R.M. (1987). Obstetric complications, neurodevelopmental deviance and risk of schizophrenia. *Journal of Psychiatric Research*, 21, 413–421.

Liberman, R.P., De Risi, W.J., & Mueser, K.T. (1989). *Social skills training for psychiatric patients*. New York: Pergamon Press.

Liberman, R.P., Spalding, W.D., & Corrigan, P.W. (1995). Cognitive-behavioural therapies in psychiatric rehabilitation. In S.R. Hirsch, & D.R. Weinberger (Eds), *Schizophrenia*. Oxford: Blackwell Science.

Liddle, P.F. (1987). The symptoms of chronic schizophrenia: A re-examination of the positive–negative dichotomy. *British Journal of Psychiatry*, 151, 145–151.

Liddle, P.F. (1996). Functional imaging: Schizophrenia. *British Medical Bulletin*, 52, 486–494.

Liddle, P.F., Friston, K.J., Frith, C.D., Hirsch, S.R., Jones, T., & Frackowiak, R.S.J. (1992). Patterns of cerebral blood flow in schizophrenia. *British Journal of Psychiatry*, 160, 179–186.

Lidz, T., Blatt, S., & Cook, B. (1981). Critique of the Danish-American studies of the adopted-away offspring of schizophrenic parents. *American Journal of Psychiatry*, 138, 1063–1067.

Lidz, T., Hotchkiss, G., & Greenblatt, M. (1957). Patient–family hospital interrelationships: Some general considerations. In M. Greenblatt, D.J. Levinson, & R.H. Williams (Eds), *The patient and the mental hospital*. Glencoe, IL: Free Press.

Lieberman, J., Jody, D., Geisler, S. et al. (1993). Time-course and biologic correlates of treatment response in 1st-episode schizophrenia. *Archives of General Psychiatry, 50*, 369–376.

Linn, M.W., Caffey, E.M., Klett, J., Hogarty, G.E., & Lamb, H.R. (1979). Day treatment and psychotropic drugs in the aftercare of schizophrenic patients: A Veterans Administration cooperative study. *Archives of General Psychiatry, 36*, 1055–1066.

Linszen, D., Dingemans, P., & Lenior, M. (1994). Cannabis abuse and the course of schizophrenic disorders. *Archives of General Psychiatry, 51*, 273–279.

Loebel, A.D., Lieberman, J.A., Alvir, J.M.J., Mayerhoff, D.I., Geisler, S.H., & Szymanski, S.R. (1992). Duration of psychosis and outcome in first-episode schizophrenia. *American Journal of Psychiatry, 149*, 1183–1188.

Lowing, P.A., Mirsky, A.F., & Pereira, R. (1983). The inheritance of schizophrenic spectrum disorders: A reanalysis of the Danish adoptive study data. *American Journal of Psychiatry, 140*, 1167–1171.

Lytton, H. (1977). Do parents create, or respond to, differences in twins? *Developmental Psychology, 13*, 456–459.

Machón, R.A., Mednick, S.A., & Schulsinger, F. (1983). The interaction of seasonality, place of birth, genetic risk and subsequent schizophrenia in a high risk sample. *British Journal of Psychiatry, 143*, 383–388.

MacMillan, J.F., Gold, A., Crow, T.J., Johnson, A.L., & Johnstone, E.C. (1986). Expressed emotion and relapse. *British Journal of Psychiatry, 148*, 133–143.

Maher, B.A. (1974). Delusional thinking and perceptual disorder. *Journal of Individual Psychology, 30*, 98–113.

Maher, B.A. (1988). Anomalous experience and delusional thinking: The logic of explanations. In T.F. Oltreanns, & B.A. Maher (Eds), *Delusional beliefs*. New York: Wiley.

Malla, A.K., Ashok, K., Norman, R.M., Williamson, P., Cortese, L., & Diaz, F. (1993). Three syndrome concepts of schizophrenia: A factor analytic study. *Schizophrenia Research, 10*, 143–150.

Malla, A.K., Cortese, L., Shaw, T.S., & Ginsberg, B. (1990). Life events and relapse in schizophrenia: A one-year prospective study. *Social Psychiatry and Psychiatric Epidemiology, 25*, 221–224.

Malla, A.K., & Norman, R.M.G. (1994). Prodromal symptoms in schizophrenia. *British Journal of Psychiatry, 164*, 487–493.

Manschreck, T.C. (1979). The assessment of paranoid features. *Comprehensive Psychiatry, 20*, 370–377.

Marder, S.R. (2000). Newer antipsychotics. *Current Opinion in Psychiatry, 13*, 11–14.

Marder, S.R., Van Putten, T., Mintz, J., Lebell, M., McKenzie, J., Faltico, G. (1984). Maintenance therapy in schizophrenia: New findings. In J. Kane (Ed.), *Drug maintenance strategies in schizophrenia* (pp. 31–49). Washington, DC: American Psychiatric Press.

Marder, S.R., Van Putten, T., Mintz, J., Lebell, M., McKenzie, J., & May, P.R. (1987). Low- and conventional-dose maintenance therapy with fluphenazine decanoate: Two-year outcome. *Archives of General Psychiatry, 44*, 518–521.

Marder, S.R., Wirshing, W.C., Van Putten, T., Mintz, J., McKenzie, J., Johnston-Cronk, K., Lebell, M., & Liberman, R.P. (1994). Fluphenazine vs placebo supplementation for prodromal signs of relapse in schizophrenia. *Archives of General Psychiatry, 51*, 280–287.

Margo, A., Hemsley, D.R., & Slade, P.D. (1981). The effects of varying auditory input on schizophrenic hallucinations. *British Journal of Psychiatry, 139*, 122–127.

Marks, I., Connolly, J.M., & Muijen, M. (1988). The Maudsley daily living programme. *Bulletin of the Royal College of Psychiatry, 12*, 22–24.

Marneros, A., Steinmeyer, E.M., Deister, A., Rohde, A., & Jünemann, H. (1989).

Long-term outcome of schizoaffective and schizophrenic disorders: A comparative study. III. Social consequences. *European Archives of Psychiatry and Neurological Science, 238,* 135–139.

McEvoy, J.P., Hogarty, G.E., & Steingard, S. (1991). Optimal dose of neuroleptic in acute schizophrenia: A controlled study of the neuroleptic threshold and higher haloperidol dose. *Archives of General Psychiatry, 48,* 739–745.

McGhie, A., & Chapman, J. (1961). Disorders of attention and perception in early schizophrenia. *British Journal of Medical Psychology, 34,* 103–116.

McGlashen, T. (1988). A selective review of North American long-term follow-up of studies of schizophrenia. *Schizophrenia Bulletin, 14,* 515–542.

McGorry, P.D. (1992). The concept of recovery and secondary prevention in psychotic disorders. *Australian and New Zealand Journal of Psychiatry, 26,* 3–18.

McGorry, P.D., Edwards, J., Mihalopoulos, C., Harringan, S.M., & Jackson, H.J. (1996). EPPIC: An evolving system of early detection and optimal management. *Schizophrenia Bulletin, 22,* 305–326.

McGorry, P.D., & Jackson, H.J. (1999). *The recognition and management of early psychosis: A preventative approach.* Cambridge: Cambridge University Press.

McGuffin, P., Sargeant, M.P., Hetti, G., Tidmarsh, S., Whatley, S., & Marchbanks, R.M. (1990). Exclusion of a schizophrenia susceptibility gene from the chromosome 5q11-q13 region: New data and a reanalysis of previous reports. *American Journal of Human Genetics, 47,* 524–535.

McGuire, P.K., Shah, G.M., & Murray, R.M. (1993). Increased blood flow in Broca's area during auditory hallucinations in schizophrenia. *Lancet, 342*(8873), 703–706.

McKenna, P.J. (1997). *Schizophrenia and related syndromes.* Hove, UK: Psychology Press.

Mednick, S.A., Machón, R.A., Huttunen, M.O., & Bonnett, D. (1988). Adult schizophrenia following prenatal exposure to an influenza epidemic. *Archives of General Psychiatry, 45,* 189–192.

Meehl, P.E. (1962). Schizotaxia, schizotypy, schizophrenia. *American Psychologist, 17,* 827–838.

Meltzer, H.Y. (1999) Risperidone and clozapine for treatment-resistant schizophrenia. *American Journal of Psychiatry, 156,* 1126–1127.

Miller, F.E. (1996). Grief therapy for relatives of persons with serious mental illness. *Psychiatric Services, 47,* 633–637.

Miller, F.E., Dworkin, J., Ward, M. et al. (1991). A preliminary study of unresolved grief in families of seriously mentally ill patients. *Hospital and Community Psychiatry, 41.*

Modestin, J. (1998). Criminal and violent behaviour in schizophrenic patients: An overview. *Psychiatry and Clinical Neurosciences, 52*(6), 547–554.

Morrison, A.P., & Haddock, G. (1997). Cognitive factors in source monitoring and auditory hallucinations. *Psychological Medicine, 27*(3), 669–679.

Morrison, R.L., & Bellack, A.S. (1984). Social skills training. In A.S. Bellack (Ed.), *Schizophrenia: Treatment, management and rehabilitation.* Orlando, FL: Grune & Stratton.

Mortonsen, P.B., Pedersen, C.B., Westergaard, T. et al. (1999). Effects of family history and place and season of birth on the risk of schizophrenia. *New England Journal of Medicine, 340,* 603–608.

Mueser, K.T., & Bellack, A.S. (1998). Social skills and social functioning. In K.T. Mueser, & N. Tarrier (Eds), *Handbook of social functioning in schizophrenia.* Boston: Allyn & Bacon.

Mueser, K.T., Bellack, A.S., Morrison, R.L., & Wade, J.H. (1990). Gender, social competence and symptomatology in schizophrenia: A longitudinal analysis. *Journal of Abnormal Psychology, 99,* 138–147.

Mueser, K.T., Bond, G.R., Drake, R.E., & Resnick, S.G. (1998). Models of community care for severe mental illness: A review of research on case management. *Schizophrenia Bulletin, 24,* 37–74.

Muijen, M. (1992). Community care: An evaluation. In D. Kavanagh (Ed.), *Schizophrenia: An overview and practical handbook.* London: Chapman & Hall.

Muijen, M., & Hadley, T. (1995). Community care: Parts and systems. In S.R. Hirsch, & D.R. Weinberger (Eds), *Schizophrenia.* Oxford: Blackwell Science.

Murphy, H.B. (1978). Cultural influences on incidence, course, and treatment response. In L.C. Wynne, R.L. Cromwell, & S. Matthysse (Eds), *The nature of schizophrenia.* New York: Wiley.

Murphy, H.B., & Rahman, A.C. (1971). The chronicity of schizophrenia in indigenous tropical peoples. *British Journal of Psychiatry, 118,* 489–497.

Nasrallah, H.A., Olson, S.C., McCalley-Whitters, M., Chapman, S., & Jacoby, G.G. (1986). Cerebral ventricular enlargement in schizophrenia: A preliminary follow up study. *Archives of General Psychiatry, 43,* 157–159.

Naylor, G.J., & Scott, C.R. (1980). Depot injections for affective disorders. *British Journal of Psychiatry, 136,* 105.

Nicole, L., Lesage, A., & Lalonde, P. (1992). Lower incidence and increased male:female ratio in schizophrenia. *British Journal of Psychiatry, 161,* 556–557.

O'Callaghan, E., Gibson, T., & Colohan, H.A. (1992). Risk of schizophrenia in adults born after obstetric complications and their association with early onset on illness: A controlled study. *British Medical Journal, 305,* 1256–1259.

Ogawa, K., Miya, M., Watari, A., Nakazawa, M., Yuasa, S., & Utena, H. (1987). A long-term follow-up study of schizophrenia in Japan with special reference to the course of social adjustment. *British Journal of Psychiatry, 151,* 758–765.

Ohouha, D.C., Hyde, T.M., & Kleinman, J.E. (1993). The role of serotonin in schizophrenia: An overview of the nomenclature, distribution and alterations of serotonin receptors in the central nervous system. *Psychopharmacology, 112,* S5–S15.

Onstad, S., Skre, I., Torgrersen, S., & Kringlen, E. (1991). Twin concordance for DSM-IIIR schizophrenia. *Acta Psychiatrica Scandinavica, 83,* 395–402.

Onyett, S. (1992). *Case management in mental health.* London: Chapman & Hall.

Owen, M.J., Lewis, S.W., & Murray, R.M. (1988). Obstetric complications and schizophrenia: A computed tomographic study. *Psychological Medicine, 18,* 331–339.

Owen, M.J., & McGuffin, P. (1991). DNA and classical genetic markers in schizophrenia. *European Achives of Psychiatry and Clinical Neuroscience, 240,* 197–203.

Patterson, P., Birchwood, M.,, & Cochrane, R. (2000) Preventing the entrenchment of high expressed emotion in first episode psychosis: early developmental attachment pathways. *Australian and New Zealand Journal of Psychiatry, 34*(Suppl.), S191–S197.

Paul, B.D. (1967). Mental disorder and self-regulating processes in culture: A Guatemalan illustration. In R. Hunt (Ed.), *Personalities and cultures: Readings in psychological anthropology.* Garden City, New York: Natural History Press.

Pearlson, G.D., Tune, L.E., Wong, D.F.,

Aylwand, E.H., Barta, P.E., Powers, R.E., Tien, A.Y., Chase, G.A., Harris, G.J., & Rabins, P.V. (1993). Quantitative $D_2$ dopamine receptor PET and structural MRI changes in late onset schizophrenia. *Schizophrenia Bulletin, 19*, 783–795.

Penn, D.L., Corrigan, P.W., Bentall, R.P., Racestein, J.H.M., & Newman, L. (1997). Social cognition in schizophrenia. *Psychological Bulletin, 121*, 114–132.

Pepper, B., Kirschner, M., & Rylewics, H. (1981). The young adult chronic patient: Overview of a population. *Hospital Community Psychiatry, 32*, 463–469.

Perry, T.L., Kish, S.J., Buchanan, J., & Hansen, S. (1979). Aminobutyric-acid deficiency in brain of schizophrenic patients. *Lancet*, 237–239.

Peters, E., Day, S., McKenna, J., & Orbach, G. (1999). Delusional ideation in religious and psychotic populations. *British Journal of Clinical Psychology, 38*(1), 83–96.

Peterson, C., Semmel, A., Von Baeyer, C., Abramson, C., Metalsky, G.I., & Seligman, M.E.P. (1982). The attributional style questionnaire. *Cognitive Therapy and Research, 3*, 287–300.

Pilgrim, D. (1990). Completing histories of madness: Some implications for modern psychiatry. In R. Bentall (Ed.), *Reconstructing schizophrenia*. London: Routledge.

Potkin, S.G., Weinberger, D.R., Linnoila, M., & Wyatt, R.J. (1983). Low CSF 5-hydroxyindoleacetic acid in schizophrenic patients with enlarged ventricles. *American Journal of Psychiatry, 140*, 21–25.

Priebe, S., Warner, R., Hubschmid, T., & Eckle, I. (1998). Employment attitudes towards work and quality of life among people with schizophrenia in three countries. *Schizophrenia Bulletin, 24*(3), 469–478.

Rachman, S.J. (1998). *Anxiety*. Hove, UK: Psychology Press.

Raine, A., Lencz, T., & Mednick, S.A. (Eds). (1995). *Schizotypal personality*. Cambridge: Cambridge University Press.

Randolph, E.T. (1998). Social networks and schizophrenia. In K.T. Mueser, & N. Tarrier (Eds), *Handbook of social functioning in schizophrenia*. Boston: Allyn & Bacon.

Rawlings, D., & Freeman, J.L. (1996). A questionnaire for the measurement of paranoia/suspiciousness. *British Journal of Clinical Psychology, 35*, 451–461.

Raz, S., & Raz, N. (1990). Structural brain abnormalities in the major psychoses: A quantative review of the evidence from computerized imagery. *Psychological Bulletin, 108*, 93–108.

Reveley, A.M., Reveley, M.A., Clifford, C.A., & Murray, R.M. (1982). Cerebral ventricular size in twins discordant for schizophrenia. *Lancet* (March), 540–541.

Ritchie, J.H., Dick, D., & Lingham, R. (1994). *The report of the inquiry into the care and treatment of Christopher Clunis*. London: HMSO.

Robinson, G.K., Bergman, G.T., & Scallet, C.J. (1989). *Choices in case management: A review of current knowledge and practice for mental health programs*. Rockville, MD: National Institute.

Rosenhan, D.L. (1973). On being sane in insane places. *Science, 179*, 250–258.

Rosenhan, D.L., & Seligman, M.I. (1988). *Abnormal psychology*. New York: Norton.

Rosenthal, D., Wender, P.H., Kety, S.S., Schulsinger, F., Welner, J., & Ostergaard, L. (1968). Schizophrenics offspring reared in adoptive homes. In D. Rosenthal & S.S. Kety (Eds), *The transmission of schizophrenia* (pp. 377–391). Oxford: Pergamon Press.

Roy, A. (1986). Suicide in schizophrenia. In A. Roy (Ed.), *Suicide*. Baltimore: Williams & Wilkins.

Roy, A., Thompson, R., & Kennedy, S. (1983). Depression in chronic schizophrenia. *British Journal of Psychiatry, 142,* 465–470.

Rüdin, E. (1916). *Zur Vererbung and Nuenentstehung der Dementia Praecox.* Berlin: Springer-Verlag.

Rutter, M., & Brown, G.W. (1966). Families containing a psychiatric patient. *Social Psychiatry, 1,* 39–52.

Rutter, M., & Sroufe, L.A. (2000). Developmental psychopathology: Concepts and challenges. *Developmental Psychopathology, 12,* 265–296.

Salokangas, R. (1983). Prognostic implications of the vex of schizophrenic patients. *British Journal of Psychiatry, 142,* 145–151.

Sameroff, A.J., & Chandler, M.J. (1975). Reproductive risk and the continuum of caretaker casualty. In F.D. Horowitz, M. Hetherington, S. Scarr-Salapatek, & G. Siegal (Eds), *Review of child development research* (Vol. 4). Chicago: Chicago University Press.

Sands, J.R., & Harrow, M. (1994). Depression during the longitudinal course of schizophrenia. *Schizophrenia Bulletin, 25*(1), 157–171.

Sartorius, N., Jablensky, A., Ernberg, G., Leff, J., Korten, A., & Gulbinat, W. (1997). Course of schizophrenia in different countries: Some results of a WHO international comparative 5 year follow-up study. In M. Hufuer, W.F. Gothax, & W. Janzarick (Eds), *Search for the causes of schizophrenia* (Vol. 1, pp. 107–113). Berlin: Springer.

Sartorius, N., Jablensky, A., Korten, A., Ernberg, G., Anker, M., Cooper, J.E., & Day, R. (1986). Early manifestations and first-contact of schizophrenia in different cultures. *Psychological Medicine, 16,* 909–928.

Scarr, S., Carter, P., & Saltzman, L. (1979). Twin method: Defence of a critical assumption. *Behaviour Genetics, 9,* 527–542.

Scazufca, M., & Kuipers, E. (1996). Links between expressed emotion and burden of care in relatives of patients with schizophrenia. *British Journal of Psychiatry, 168,* 580–587.

Scazufca, M., & Kuipers, E. (1998). Stability of expressed emotion in relatives of those with schizophrenia and its relationship with burden of care and perception of patients' social functioning. *Psychological Medicine, 28,* 453–461.

Schneider, K. (1959). *Clinical psychopathology.* New York: Grune & Stratton.

Scull, A. (1979). *Measures of madness.* London: Allen Lane.

Scull, A. (1983). Humanitarianism or control? Some observations on the historiography of Anglo-American psychiatry. In S. Cohen, & A. Scull (Eds), *Social control and the state.* Oxford: Blackwell.

Sedgwick, P. (1982). *Psycho politics.* Chichester, UK: Wiley.

Seeman, M.V. (1982). Gender differences in schizophrenia. *Canadian Journal of Psychiatry, 27,* 107–112.

Seeman, P., Hong-Chang, G., & Van Tol, H.H.M. (1993). Dopamine D4 receptors elevated in schizophrenia. *Nature, 365,* 441–445.

Sham, P.C., O'Callaghan, E., Takei, N., Murray, G.K., Hare, E.H., & Murray, R.M. (1992). Schizophrenia following prenatal exposure to influenza epidemics between 1939 and 1960. *British Journal of Psychiatry, 160,* 461–466.

Sharma, T., du Boulay, G., Lewis, S., Sigmundsson, T., Gurling, H., & Murray, R.M. (1997). The Maudlsey Family study: I. Structural brain changes on magnetic resonance imaging in familial schizophrenia. *Progress in Neuro-Pharmacology & Biological Psychiatry, 21,* 1297–1315.

Sharp, M.M., Fear, C.F., & Healy, D. (1997).

Attributional style and delusions: An investigation based on delusional content. *European Psychiatry, 12,* 1–7.

Shepherd, G. (1977). Social skills training: The generalization problem. *Behaviour Therapy, 8,* 1008–1009.

Shepherd, G. (1998). Models of community care. *Journal of Mental Health, 7,* 165–177.

Shepherd, M., Watt, D., Falloon, I.R., & Smeeton, N. (1989a). The natural history of schizophrenia: A five-year follow up study of outcome and prediction in a representative sample of schizophrenics. *Psychological Medicine* (Monograph Suppl. 15, pp. 1–46).

Sherrington, R., Brynjolfsson, J., Petursson, H., Potter, M., Dudleston, K., Barraclough, B., Wasmuth, J., Dobbs, M., & Gurling, H. (1988). Localization of a susceptibility locus for schizophrenia on chromosome 5. *Nature, 336,* 164–167.

Sims, A. (1991). Delusional syndromes in ICD-10. *British Journal of Psychiatry, 159*(Suppl. 14), 46–51.

Singer, M.T., & Wynne, L.C. (1963). Differentiating characteristics of parents of childhood schizophrenics, childhood neurotics and young adult schizophrenics. *American Journal of Psychiatry, 120,* 234–243.

Siris, S.G. (1995). Depression and schizophrenia. In S.R. Hirsch, & D.R. Weinberger (Eds), *Schizophrenia.* Oxford: Blackwell Science.

Slade, P.D. (1973). The psychological investigation and treatment of auditory hallucinations: A second case report. *British Journal of Medical Psychology, 46,* 293–296.

Slade, P.D., & Bentall, R.P. (1988). *Sensory deceptions: A scientific analysis of hallucination.* Baltimore: Johns Hopkins University Press.

Slater, E., & Cowie, V. (1971). *The genetics of mental disorders.* London: Oxford University Press.

Smith, C. (1970). Heritability of liability

and concordance in monzygous twins. *Annals of Human Genetics, 34,* 578–588.

Smith, J., & Birchwood, M.J. (1990). Relatives and patients as partners in the management of schizophrenia: The development of a service model. *British Journal of Psychiatry, 156,* 654–660.

Smith, J., Birchwood, M.J., Cochrane, R., & George, S. (1993). The needs of high and low expressed emotion families: A normative approach. *Social Psychiatry and Psychiatric Epidemiology, 28,* 11–16.

Spitzer, R.L., Endicott, J., & Robins, E. (1978). Research diagnostic criteria: Rationale and reliability. *Archives of General Psychiatry, 35,* 773–782.

Spitzer, R.I., & Fleiss, J.L. (1974). A reanalysis of the reliability of psychiatric diagnosis. *British Journal of Psychiatry, 123,* 341–347.

Stein, C.J., & Test, M.A. (1980). Alternative to mental hospital treatment: A conceptual model treatment program and clinical evaluation. *Archives of General Psychiatry, 37,* 392–397.

Stirling, J., Tantam, D., Newby, D. et al. (1993). Expressed emotion and schizophrenia: The ontogeny of EE during an 18 month follow-up. *Psychological Medicine, 23,* 771–778.

Stirling, J., Tantam, D., Thonks, P., Newby, D., & Montague, L. (1991). Expressed emotion and early onset schizophrenia. *Psychological Medicine, 21,* 675–685.

Strauss, J.S. (1969). Hallucinations and delusions as points on continuum functions. *Archives of General Psychiatry, 21,* 581–586.

Strauss, J.S., & Carpenter, W.T. (1972). Prediction of outcome in schizophrenia: Characteristics of outcome. *Archives of General Psychiatry, 27,* 739–746.

Strauss, J.S., & Carpenter, W.T. (1977). Prediction of outcome in schizophrenia: II. Relationship between predictor and outcome variables. *Archives of General Psychiatry, 31,* 37–42.

Sturt, E. (1981). Hierarchical patterns in the

distribution of psychiatric symptoms. *Psychological Medicine, II*, 783–794.

Subotnik, K.L., & Nuechterlein, K.H. (1988). Prodromal signs and symptoms of schizophrenic relapse. *Journal of Abnormal Psychology, 97*, 405–412.

Suddath, R.L., Christison, G.W., Torrey, E.F. et al. (1990). Anatomical abnormalities in the brains of monozygotic twins discordant for schizophrenia. *New England Journal of Medicine, 322*, 789–794.

Sumiyoshi, T., Hasegawa, M., Jayathilake, K. et al. (1990). Sex differences in plasma homovanillic acid levels in schizophrenia and normal controls: Relation to neuroleptic resistance. *Biological Psychiatry, 41*, 560–566.

Suzuki, M., Yuasa, S., Minabi, Y., Murata, M., & Kurachi, M. (1993). Left superior temporal blood flow increases in schizophrenic and schizophreniform patients with auditory hallucinations: A longitudinal case study using [123]I-IMPSPECT. *European Archives of Psychiatry and Clinical Neuroscience, 242*, 257–261.

Szasz, T.D. (1979). *Schizophrenia: The sacred symbol of psychiatry*. London: Oxford University Press.

Szeszko, P.R., Bilder, R.M., Wu, H. et al. (1995). Reduced mesiotemporal lobe volumes and asymmetries in schizophrenia. *Biological Psychiatry, 37*, 671–671.

Tamminga, C.A., Crayton, J.W., & Chase, T.N. (1978). Muscimol: GABA agonist therapy in schizophrenia. *American Journal of Psychiatry, 135*, 746–747.

Tarrier, N. (1987). An investigation of residual psychotic symptoms in discharged schizophrenic patients. *British Journal of Clinical Psychology, 26*, 141–143.

Tarrier, N., Barrowclough, C., Vaughn, C., Bamrah, J.S., Porceddu, K., Watts, S., & Freeman, H. (1988). The community management of schizophrenia: A controlled trial of a behavioural intervention with families to reduce relapse. *British Journal of Psychiatry, 153*, 532–542.

Tarrier, N., Barrowclough, C., Vaughn, C., Bamrah, J.S., Porceddu, K., Watts, S., & Freeman, H. (1989). Community management of schizophrenia: A two-year follow-up of a behavioural intervention with families. *British Journal of Psychiatry, 154*, 625–628.

Tarrier, N., Beckett, R., Harwood, S. et al. (1993). A trial of two cognitive-behavioural methods of treating drug-resistant residual psychotic symptoms in schizophrenic patients: I. Outcome. *British Journal of Psychiatry, 162*, 524–532.

Tesser, A., & Shaffer, D.R. (1990). Attitudes and attitude change. *Annual Review of Psychology, 41*, 479–523.

Thara, R., Henrietta, M., Joseph, A. et al. (1994). Ten-year course of schizophrenia – the Madras longitudinal study. *Acta Psychiatrica Scandinavica, 90*, 329–336.

Thornicroft, G., & Breakey, W. (1991). The COSTAR Program I: Improving social networks of the long-term mentally ill. *British Journal of Psychiatry, 159*, 245–259.

Tienari, P., Wynne, L.C., Moring, J. et al. (1994). The Finnish adoptive family study of schizophrenia: Implications for family research. *British Journal of Psychiatry* (Suppl. 23), 20–26.

Torrey, E.F., Bowler, A.E., Taylor, E.H., & Gottesman, I.I. (1990). *Schizophrenia and manic depression disorders: The biological roots of mental illness as revealed by a landmark study of identical twins*. New York: Basic Books.

Trower, P., Bryant, B., & Argyle, M. (1978). *Social skills and mental health*. London: Methuen.

Trower, P., & Chadwick, P. (1995). Pathways to defence of the self: A theory of two types of paranoia. *Clinical*

*Psychology: Science and Practice*, *2*, 263–278.

Tsuang, M.T., Woolson, R.F., & Fleming, J.A. (1979). Long term outcome of major psychoses: I. Schizophrenia and affective disorders compared with psychiatrically symptom free surgical conditions. *Archives of General Psychiatry*, *36*, 1295–1301.

Vaughn, C.E. and Leff, J. (1976). The influence of family and social factors on the course of psychiatric illness. *British Journal of Psychiatry*, *129*, 125–137.

Ventura, J., Nuechterlein, K.H., Hardistry, J.P., & Gittin, M. (1992). Life events and schizophrenic relapse after withdrawal of medication: A prospective study. *British Journal of Psychiatry*, *161*, 615–620.

Vita, A., Sacchetti, G., & Cazullo, C.L. (1988). Brain morphology in schizophrenia: A 2- to 5-year follow up study. *Acta Psychiatrica Scandinavica*, *78*, 618–621.

Walker, E., & Lewine, R.J. (1990). Prediction of adult-onset schizophrenia from childhood home movies of the patients. *American Journal of Psychiatry*, *147*, 1052–1056.

Wang, Z.W., Black, D., Andreasen, N., & Crowe, R.R. (1993). A linkage study of chromosome 11q in schizophrenia. *Archives of General Psychiatry*, *50*, 212–216.

Warner, R. (1994). *Recovery from schizophrenia: Psychiatry and political economy*. London: Routledge.

Watts, F.N., Powell, E.G., Austin, S.V. (1973). The modification of abnormal beliefs. *British Journal of Medical Psychology*, *46*, 359–363.

Waxler, N.E. (1979). Is outcome for schizophrenia better in non-industrial societies? The case of Sri Lanka. *Journal of Nervous and Mental Disease*, *167*, 144–158.

Weinberger, D.R. (1987). Implications of normal brain development for the pathogenesis of schizophrenia. *Archives of General Psychiatry*, *44*, 660–669.

Weinberger, D.R., Berman, K.F., & Zec, R.F. (1986). Physiologic dysfunction of dorsolateral prefrontal cortex in schizophrenia: I. Regional cerebral blood flow evidence. *Archives of General Psychiatry*, *43*, 114–124.

Weller, M.P.I. (1989). Mental illness: Who cares? *Nature*, *339*, 249–252.

Wender, P.H., Rosenthal, D., Kety, S.S., Schulsinger, F., & Weiner, J. (1974). Cross-fostering: A research strategy for clarifying the role of genetic and experimental factors in the etiology of schizophrenia. *Archives of General Psychiatry*, *30*, 121–128.

Wig, N.N., Menon, D.K., Bedi, M., Leff, J., Kuipers, L., Ghosh, A., Day, R., Korten, A., Ernberg, G., Sartorius, N. (1987). Expressed emotion and schizophrenia in North India: II. Distribution of expressed emotion components among relatives of schizophrenic patients in Aarhus and Chandigarh. *British Journal of Psychiatry*, *151*, 160–165.

Wing, J.K. (1992). Differential diagnosis of schizophrenia. In L.D. Kavanagh (Ed.), *Schizophrenia: An overview and practical handbook*. London: Chapman & Hall.

Wing, J.K., Bennett, D.H., & Denham, J. (1964). The industrial rehabilitation of long stay schizophrenic patients. *Medical Research Council Memo 42*. London: HMSO.

Wing, J.K., & Brown, G.W. (1970). *Institutionalism and schizophrenia: A comparative study of mental hospitals, 1960–1968*. Cambridge: Cambridge University Press.

Winokur, G., Scharfetter, C., & Angst, J. (1985). The diagnostic value in assessing mood congruence in delusions and hallucinations and their relationship to the affective state. *European Archives of Psychiatry and Neurological Science*, *234*, 299–302.

Winters, K.C., & Neale, J.M. (1983).

Delusions and delusional thinking in psychotics: A review of the literature. *Clinical Psychology Review, 3,* 227–253.

Wise, C.D., & Stein, L. (1973). Dopamine–hydroxylase deficits in the brains of schizophrenic patients. *Science, 181,* 344–347.

Wooley, D.W., & Shaw, E. (1954). A biochemical and pharmacological suggestion about certain mental disorders. *Proceedings of the National Academy of Sciences, 40,* 228.

Worland, J., Weeks, D.G., Janes, C.L., & Strock, B.D. (1984). Intelligence, classroom behavior, and academic achievement in children at high and low risk for psychopathology: A structural equation analysis. *Journal of Abnormal Child Psychology, 12,* 437–454.

World Health Organisation (1973). *The international pilot study of schizophrenia.* Geneva: WHO.

World Health Organisation (1979). *Schizophrenia: An international follow-up study.* New York: Wiley.

World Health Organisation (1992). *The ICD-10 Classification of mental and behavioural disorders: Clinical descriptors and diagnosis guidelines.* Geneva: WHO.

Wright, P., Murray, R.M., Donaldson, P.T., & Underhill, J.A. (1993). Do maternal HLA antigens predispose to schizophrenia? *Lancet, 342,* 117–118.

Wyatt, R.J., Schwarz, M.A., Erdelyi, E., & Barchas, J.D. (1975). Dopamine-hydroxylase activity in brains of chronic schizophrenic patients. *Science, 187,* 368–370.

Young, H.F., Bentall, R.P., Slade, P.D., & Dewey, M.E. (1987). The role of brief instructions and suggestibility in the elicitation of auditory and visual hallucinations in normal and psychiatric subjects. *Journal of Nervous and Mental Disease, 5,* 41–48.

Zhang, M., Wang, M., Li, J. et al. (1995). Randomised-control trial of family intervention for 78 first-episode male schizophrenic patients: An 18-month study in Suzhou, Jiangsu. *British Journal of Psychiatry* (Suppl. 24), 96–102.

Ziegler, E., & Glick, M. (1988). Is paranoid schizophrenia really camouflaged depression? *American Psychologist, 43,* 284–290.

Zimbado, P.G., Anderson, S.M., & Kabat, L.G. (1981). Induced hearing deficit generates experimental paranoia. *Science, 212,* 1529–1531.

Zubin, J., Magaziler, J., & Heinhauser, S.R. (1983). The metamorphosis of schizophrenia: From chronicity to vulnerability. *Psychological Medicine, 13,* 551–571.

Zubin, J., & Spring, B. (1977). Vulnerability: A new view of schizophrenia. *Journal of Abnormal Psychology, 86,* 103–126.

# Author Index

Wooley, D.W. 53  
Woolson, R.F. 25  
Worland, J. 46  
World Health Organisation  
10, 17, 26, 27, 31, 32, 67, 78,  
79, 82, 88  

Wright, P. 50  
Wyatt, R.J. 53  
Wynne, L.C. 42, 46, 69, 70  

Young, H.F. 89  
Yuasa, S. 60  

Zec, R.F. 60  
Zhang, M. 131  
Ziegler, E. 85  
Zimbado, P.G. 87  
Zisook, S. 56  
Zubin, J. 26, 63

# Subject Index

Charpentier 99

child development, transactional models 73

childhood precursors 45–51; attentional difficulties 46; emotional difficulties 46, 48, 50; information processing difficulties 46; IQ scores 46; locus of control 46; neurodevelopmental theories 47–53, 56–7; neuromotor abnormalities 47; psychosocial difficulties 46, 48, 50; retrospective studies 47; self-esteem 46; verbal function 46, 48; withdrawal 48

chlorpromazine 99; *see also* medication

clinical trials: cognitive-behavioural therapy 120, 132; cognitive therapy 123; controls, experimental 66; drop-out rates 120, 127, 128; medication 100, 102; *see also* research studies

clozapine 4, 104; *see also* medication

Clunis, Christopher *see* violence, risk of

cognitive-behavioural therapy 117–20; coping strategy enhancement (CSE) 119, 120; problem solving therapy 120; trials 120, 132

cognitive therapy 5, 117, 121–4; defining 121; education and rapport training 121; effectiveness of 123; empirical testing 121, 122–3; research trials 123; uses 121

Colin (case study) 3, 4, 7, 8

community care 112–15, 116; assertive community treatment model (ACT) 114, 115; assessing 115; benefits of 113, 115, 116;

expanded broker model 114; loss of contact 115; personal strengths model 114; problems of 113, 115; rehabilitation approach 114; and violent crime 6, 113, 115

community outreach, assertive 5

community psychiatric nurse (CPN) 114

comorbidity 32–3

computerised tomography (CT) 55, 57

confidence, loss of 20

conflict management 109

continuum theory 13, 14, 37, 42–3, 95–6

control, delusions of 1, 2, 3, 7, 8, 92

conversational training 108–10

coping strategies 117–19, 132; attention narrowing 118; breathing exercises 119; for delusions 117, 118; distraction 118, 119; families 77, 129; initiating social contact 118; multiple 119; positive self-talk 118; relaxation exercises 119; success of 119; for voices 89; withdrawal 118, 119

coping strategy enhancement (CSE) 119, 120; assessing responses 119; assessing symptoms 119; collaborative empiricism 119, 120; education and rapport training 119; evaluating 120; symptom targeting 120

corpus callosum 56

cortex 56, 57, 58, 60; asymmetry 57

criticism *see* expressed emotion (EE) studies

cultural factors 26–8; and diagnosis 27; and employment 27, 80, 81, 82;

explaining 79, 80; family differences 27, 81; Guatemala 28; India 79; influence of 78–82; kinship ties 81; Mauritias 26; and outcomes 26–8, 34, 78, 79, 82; prevalence rates 26; social reintegration 82; Sri Lanka 27; and stress 80, 81; tolerance factors 80, 82

Danish-American Adoption Studies 41

defences: delusions as 85, 86; depressive 85

Delay 99

delusional disorder 7

delusions 1, 7, 11, 13, 17, 20; and abnormal perception 84, 87, 94, 96; and attributional style 85, 86, 87; and beliefs 84, 87, 91; of control 1, 2, 3, 7, 8, 92; coping strategies 117, 118; and data-gathering 86, 87; as defence 85, 86; definition of 2, 84; depressive 16; diagnosis of 84; generation of 70; of identity 2; inconsistent 122; irrational 122; mood congruent 17, 18; in normals 87; and outcomes 32; paranoid model 84, 85; persecutory 2, 7, 17, 18, 85, 86; psychology of 83, 84–7; and reasoning bias 84–7, 94, 96; reasoning with 121; of reference 7, 8, 17; religious 2, 8; secondary 17; and self-esteem 85, 86; and theory of mind deficiency 93; treating 87

dementia praecox 14

Deniker 99

depression, unipolar 7, 12, 13, 16, 17, 18; comorbid 32–3, 59, 117; defences against 85; delusions in 16; and outcome 32–3, 34; and

stress 65; treating 121; *see also* manic depression
developmental disorders *see* childhood precursors *and* neurodevelopmental theories
diagnosis 7, 9–14, 20; accuracy 9, 10, 13, 15, 16; categorisation 12, 13, 14; continuum theory 13, 14, 37, 42–3, 95–6; dual 113; predictive validity of 16; standardising 9, 10; US/UK diagnostic project 13
diagnostic classification systems 10; *Diagnostic and Statistical Manuals DSM - III-R 84; DSM-IV* 10, 11, 15, 20; *International Classification of Diseases ICD-10* 10, 11, 15, 20; *Research Diagnostic Criteria RDC* 10
distraction 118, 119
dopamine 24, 51, 92, 104; hypothesis 52, 53, 54; receptors 104
drug abuse *see* substance abuse
drug treatment *see* medication
dual diagnosis 113

early intervention 5, 124–9, 132
early signs scale (ESS) 126
education and rapport training 121
ego development 69, 70
emotional functioning 8, 11; blunted 17–19, 26, 32, 59; in juveniles 46, 48, 50; inappropriate responses 14, 19; labile 59; *see also* affective disorders
emotional over-involvement (EOI), families 27, 75, 77, 82; *see also* expressed emotion
employment 20, 26, 109–11; cultural differences 27, 80,

81, 82; dysfunction 11; and gender 28; job clubs 111–12; place and train 111; and premorbid functioning 30; and recovery 27, 111; supported 111, 116
environmental: deprivation 18; influences 37; overstimulation 82; risk factors 61, 71; *see also* stress *and* twin studies
epidemiology 21–34; and cultural factors 26–8; and gender 28–30; incidence 21, 33
Errol (case study) 2, 7, 8
excitation *see* psychomotor changes
expanded broker model 114
expressed emotion (EE) studies 27, 32, 129, 130, 132; cultural variations 81; studies 74–8; *see also* emotional over-involvement (EOI)

families, affect on 5–6, 77, 130; carers 70, 73, 74; coping 77, 129; grief 5, 6, 77
families, influence of 27, 31–2, 63, 82; communication within 69, 70, 130, 132; and course of illness 74–8, 82; cultural differences 27, 81; emotional over-involvement (EOI) 27, 75, 77, 82; hostility 31, 32, 77, 82, 94, 129; risk factors 35, 36, 37, 61; theories of 69–74
family interventions 117, 129–32
family socialisation theory 70
family studies 35, 36; age corrected 35; outcome studies 130–32
feelings: of alienation 33; anhedonia 18; apathy 18; symptom induced 117; *see also* emotion

flupenthixol 99; *see also* medication
fluphenazine 99, 102, 128; *see also* medication
Frith's model 92, 93

GABA 53, 54
gender: and age of onset 28, 29, 50; and brain development 50; and brain structure 56, 57; and employment 28; and outcome 28–30, 34; and social impairment 28, 29
genetics, molecular 43–5; allele-sharing 44; linkage studies 43–5

hallucinations 1, 5, 7, 11, 13, 17, 20; incidence of 16; psychology of 83, 96; *see also* auditory hallucinations
haloperidol 99, 100, 127; *see also* medication
handedness, and schizophrenia 58
Hemsley's model 93–4
heritability, of schizophrenia *see* biological models
high-risk studies 45–7, 49, 61; Israeli study 46
hippocampus 56, 94
homovanillic acid (HVA) 52
humour, losing sense of 4, 8
hypofrontality 59, 60
hypomania 12

identity, delusions of 2
*impairments: cognitive 94; intrinsic 8, 9, 20; psychological 9; secondary 8, 9, 20; social 9*
inheritance *see* biological models
institutional care 112, 113
*International Classification of Diseases ICD-10* 10, 11, 12, 15, 20
international pilot study of schizophrenia 17, 32, 78, 88

interventions: appropriate 16; early 5, 124–9, 132; cognitive-behavioural 117–20; cognitive therapy 117; family 117, 129–32; psychological 4, 5, 117–32; relapse prevention 117, 124–9, 131, 132; social 107–16

interview schedule for social interactions (ISSI) 31

interviews, semi-structured 20

Israeli High Risk Study 46

job clubs 111–12

Joe (case study) 1, 7, 8

Kasannin 13

labelling 80

Laborit 99

language see speech

largactil see chlorpromazine

liability, to schizophrenia 38–41, 43, 51, 61; see also risk

life events, and illness 64–9, 75, 82; contextual threat of 66; prospective studies 68; retrospective studies 64, 65, 66; second generation studies 67–9; as trigger 68, 95; see also stress

life events and difficulties scale (LEDS) 67, 68

lifestyle changes 33

limbic system 54, 56, 57

linkage studies 43, 44

madness, medicalisation of 14

magnetic resonance imaging (MRI) 49, 55, 57, 58

maintenance medication 101–3, 128, 129

manic depression 7, 12, 13, 14, 17

Mark (case study) 3, 7

media reporting 6

medication, neuroleptic 4, 6, 24, 99–105; acute treatment 100–101; atypical 103–4, 105; and brain chemistry 51, 52; and community care 112; dosage 100, 101; low dose 102–3; maintenance 101, 102, 103, 128, 129; for negative symptoms 104, 105; for positive symptoms 100; and relapse 64–5, 68, 75–6, 101–3, 105; resistance 104; response to 16, 50; sedative 99; self-management 109; side-effects 18, 53, 55–6, 60, 100–102, 104; stress-buffering function of 65; threshold 100; timing of 100; tolerance 104; trials 100, 102

memory: bias 85; /perceptual confusion 94, 96

midbrain structures 56

molecular genetics 43–5; allele-sharing 44; linkage studies 43–5

money management 109

monoamine oxidase (MAO) 51

mood disorders see affective disorders

motivation problems 8

motor behaviour see psychomotor changes

negative symptoms 17, 18–20, 26, 32–4; medication for 104, 105; motivation problems 8; psychomotor poverty 19, 20, 32, 59 reducing 107; self care 5; speech poverty 17, 19, 26, 32, 59; and ventricle enlargement 59; withdrawal 3, 5, 8, 17, 18, 32

neuroanatomy, abnormalities 46, 47, 49, 51, 55–7; brain size/weight 55; corpus

callosum 56; cortex 56, 57, 58, 60; cortical asymmetry 57; hippocampus 56, 94; and language 58; limbic system 54, 56, 57; midbrain structures 56; post mortem studies 51, 52, 54, 55, 56; twin studies 58; ventricle enlargement 19, 47, 49, 57, 58, 59

neurochemistry see neurotransmitters

neurodevelopmental theories 11, 45, 47–53, 56–7, 60, 61; brain lesions 48; and gender 50; perinatal and birth complications (PCB's) 49, 50, 57, 60, 61; in-utero viral infections 49, 50; verbal problems 46, 48; winter births 49; see also childhood precursors

neuro imaging studies 46, 47, 49, 51, 57–60; computerised tomography (CT) 55, 57; magnetic resonance imaging (MRI) 49, 55, 57, 58; positron emission tomography (PET) 52, 53, 57, 59; single photon emission computed tomography (SPECT) 52, 57

neuroleptic: medication see medication; threshold 100

neuropathology see neuroanatomy and brain function

neuropsychological models 83, 91–4, 96; attentional defects 92; Frith's model 92, 93; Hemsley's model 93–4; memory/perceptual confusion 94, 96

neurotransmitters 19, 51–5; amino acid 51, 53–4; dopamine 51, 52, 53, 92, 104; gamma amniobutyric acid (GABA) 53, 54; glutamate 54; monoamines 51; neuropeptides 51;

noradrenalin 51, 53;
serotonin (5-HT) 51, 53, 104
noradrenalin 51, 53

occupation *see* employment
oestrogen, protective effect of
29
olanzapine 4, 104; *see also*
medication
organic brain disease 12, 19,
46
outcomes 19; for acute onset
32; cultural differences
26–8, 34, 78, 79, 82;
delusions 32; depression
32–3, 34; family
intervention studies
130–32; gender studies
28–30; personality changes
32; premorbid functioning
as predictor of 28, 30–31,
33, 34; symptoms as
predictor of 32, 33, 34; *see
also* recovery *and* relapse

panic disorder 121
paranoid: model of delusions
84, 85; psychosis 18;
thinking 84
passivity experiences *see*
control, delusions of
perception: abnormal 14, 84,
87, 94, 96; internal/external
confusion 92
perinatal and birth
complications (PCB's) 49,
50, 57, 60, 61
persecutory delusions 2, 7, 17,
18, 85, 86; coping strategies
117, 118
personal strengths model 114
personality changes 32
Peterson 99
phenothiazines 24, 99; *see also*
medication
place and train 111
positive self-talk 118
positive symptoms 17–20, 26,
32, 50; controlling 117, 118,
120; coping strategies 117,

118, 119, 132; easing
distress 117–21, 132;
feelings induced by 117;
medicating 100;
neuropsychological models
of 83, 91–4, 96; proneness to
95–6; psychological
theories of 83–91; triggers
118, 119; *see also* delusions
*and* hallucinations
positron emission
tomography (PET) 52, 53,
57, 59
post mortem studies 51, 52,
54, 55, 56
premorbid functioning 12, 18,
21; and outcome 28, 30–31,
33, 34
primary process thinking 69
prodromal symptoms 102,
103, 124–8
prognosis *see* outcomes
promethazine 99; *see also*
medication
proneness, to psychosis *see*
schizotypy
psychiatric state examination
(PSE) 15
psychological interventions 4,
5, 117–32; cognitive-
behavioural 117–20;
cognitive therapy 117;
family intervention 117,
129–32; relapse prevention
117, 124–9, 131, 132
psychomotor changes;
excitation 5, 59; juvenile 47;
poverty 19, 20, 32, 59 ;
stereotyped behaviour 14
psychosis *see* delusions *and*
hallucinations
psychosis proneness 83, 95–6,
97
psychosocial *see* psychological
interventions
psychotic traits 96

reality: construction,
childhood 70; distortion 7,
19, 20, 59, 60; *see also*

delusions *and*
hallucinations
reasoning bias 84, 85, 86, 87,
94, 96
recovery 4, 14, 16, 21–6, 34;
and acute onset 32; and age
of onset 30; with aging 24,
26; and comorbidity 32–3,
34; complete 21; cultural
variations 26–8, 34; and
employment 27, 111;
follow-up studies 22, 23, 24;
and gender 28–30, 34; long-
term 24–6; psychological
21, 26, 34; and reintegration
28; social 21, 23, 24, 26; and
social support 27, 31–2, 34;
symptomatic 21, 26;
Vermont study 24; *see also*
outcomes
recreational skills 109
rehabilitation 24, 28, 114; *see
also* community care
relapse: early signs scale (ESS)
126; education about 125;
factors affecting 32, 33, 78;
and medication 64–5, 68,
75–6, 101–3, 105;
prevention 117, 124–9, 131,
132; process of 124;
prodromal symptoms of
102, 103, 124–8; research
trials 127–9; signature
124–8, 132; triggers of 64,
65, 68, 9
relationship: difficulties 19,
95; mother-child 69;
training 108
relaxation exercises 119
religious delusions 2, 8
remission *see* recovery *and*
relapse
*research: adoption studies 41,
71–3; cross-cultural 78;
expressed emotion (EE)
studies 74–8, family
intervention studies 130–32;
follow-up studies 22, 23, 24;
high-risk studies 45–7, 49, 61;
international pilot study of*